```
306.87                         787
Jam      James, John A.
         A Help to Domestic
           Happiness
```

A Help to Domestic Happiness

by John Angell James
(Author of *Female Piety*, *Addresses to Young Men*, and *The Christian Father's Present to His Children*)

"Behold! how good and how pleasant it is for brethren to dwell together in unity!"
"It is like the precious ointment upon the head, that ran down upon the beard, even Aaron's beard: that went down to the skirst of his garments. As the dew of Hermon, and as the dew that descended upon the mountains of Zion: for there the Lord commanded the blessing, even life forevermore."
Psalm 133

Soli Deo Gloria Publications
...for instruction in righteousness...

Library
Grace Evangelical Church
9750 Dogwood
Germantown, TN 38139

Soli Deo Gloria Publications
P.O. Box 451, Morgan, PA 15064
(412) 221-1901/FAX 221-1902

*

A Help to Domestic Happiness was first published in 1833 in London as *The Family Monitor, or A Help to Domestic Happiness* by Frederick Westley and A.H. Davis. This Soli Deo Gloria reprint is 1995. Printed in the USA.

*

ISBN 1-57358-005-8

PREFACE.

The substance of the ensuing chapters was delivered by the Author in a course of sermons which followed a series of expository lectures on the Epistle to the Ephesians. The consecutive method of preaching, which he principally uses, is attended, he thinks, with this, among many other advantages, that it brings under the review of a minister, many subjects which would otherwise be overlooked; affords an opportunity for the introduction of some topics, which, from their peculiarity, seem to require such a way of access to the pulpit; and also furnishes an apology for the discussion of others, which the fastidiousness of modern delicacy has almost excluded from the range of pastoral admonition. On entering upon the first branch of relative duties, the Author was so much under the influence, perhaps improperly, of this excess of refinement, and felt so much the difficulty of making a public statement of the duties of husbands and wives, that he had determined, at one time, to relieve himself from the embarrassment, by merely reading large extracts from Mr. Jay's beautiful sermon on this subject. After he had preached two discourses, and thus discharged, as well as he was able, this rather perplexing task, he received a numerously signed petition from many husbands and their wives, belonging to his congregation, requesting that they might be permitted to *read* in print the statement of their mutual obligations, which they had heard delivered with so much fidelity and impartiality from the pulpit. Instead of being limited by this request, the Author has gone beyond it, and sent forth the whole series of relative duties; thus furnishing a manual of advice, in which all the members of the household may find something appropriate to the peculiarity of their circumstances.

It is an unquestionable truth, that if a man be not happy at home, he cannot be happy any where ; and the converse of the proposition is no less true, that he who *is* happy there, need be miserable no where. "It is the place of all the world I love most," said the interesting Author of the Task, when speaking of home. And *he* may be felicitated who can say the same. Any attempt, however feeble, to render the domestic circle, what it ever should be, a scene of comfort, is at least benevolent. Nor is this a hopeless effort; for he who has the bible in his hand, and speaks as the oracles of God, can disclose at once, and in few words, the important secret. The principles of greatest consequence to mankind, whether we refer to science or to morals, lie not buried deep in gloom and mystery, but are to be found, like the manna of the Israelites, upon the surface of things. The secret of happiness lies folded up in the leaves of the bible, and is carried in the bosom of religion. The Author knows of no other way to felicity, and therefore does not profess to teach any other. Let the two parties in wedded life be believers in Christ Jesus, and partake themselves of the peace that passeth understanding; let them, when they become a father and a mother, bring up their children in the fear of God; and as a master and a mistress, be diligent and successful in instructing their servants in the principles of religion, and if happiness is to be found upon earth, it will be enjoyed within the hallowed circle of a family, thus united by love, and sanctified by grace.

The Author does not deny, that much of worldly comfort may be, and often is, enjoyed in some families, which neither possess nor profess a serious regard to the claims of religion; while it must be acknowledged on the other hand, that there are to be found professors of religion, whose households are any thing but happy ones. In reference to the former, it may be affirmed, that piety, while it would raise their enjoyment to a sublimer kind, and a higher degree of happiness in this world, would also perpetuate it through eternity; and in reference to the latter, it may be remarked, that their disquietude is not produced by religion, but occasioned by the want of it. A mere profession of the christian faith, is rather a hindrance to felicity than a help : nothing short of real religion can be expected to yield its joys.

In the following pages, there will be found numerous and long extracts from an incomparably excellent work, by the Rev. Christopher Anderson, of Edinburgh, entitled, "The Domestic Constitution." Of that volume, the Author feels that his own is not worthy, in any instance, to be the harbinger; but should he find that he has introduced any families to an acquaintance with a treatise, so well worthy of their most serious attention, he will be thankful for that measure of benefit, and rejoice that he has not laboured in vain.

Edgbaston, September 13, 1828.

CONTENTS.

CHAPTER I.
THE DOMESTIC CONSTITUTION 1

CHAPTER II.
THE MUTUAL DUTIES OF HUSBANDS AND WIVES 11

CHAPTER III.
THE SPECIAL DUTIES OF HUSBANDS AND WIVES 38

CHAPTER IV.
SOME REMARKS ON THE FORMATION OF THE MARRIAGE UNION 82

CHAPTER V.
THE DUTIES OF PARENTS 106

CHAPTER VI.
THE DUTIES OF CHILDREN TO THEIR PARENTS 171

CHAPTER VII.
ON THE FRATERNAL DUTIES 208

CHAPTER VIII.
THE DUTIES OF MASTERS 233

CHAPTER IX.
THE DUTIES OF SERVANTS 271

CHAPTER I.

THE DOMESTIC CONSTITUTION.

> "By Thee
> Founded in reason, loyal, just and pure,
> Relations dear, and all the charities
> Of Father, Son, and Brother, first were known.
> Far be it that I should write thee, sin or blame,
> Or think thee unbefitting holiest place,
> Perpetual fountain of domestic sweets!"
>
> MILTON.

A FAMILY! How delightful the associations we form with such a word! How pleasing the images with which it crowds the mind, and how tender the emotions which it awakens in the heart! Who can wonder that domestic happiness should be a theme dear to poetry, and that it should have called forth some of the sweetest strains of fancy and of feeling? Or who can be surprised, that of all the objects which present themselves in the vista of futurity to the eye of those who are setting out on the journey of life, this should excite the most ardent desires, and engage the most active pursuits? But alas! of those who in the ardour of youth start for the possession of this dear prize, how many fail? And why? *Because their imagination alone is engaged on the subject:* they have no definite ideas of what it means, nor of the way in which it is to be obtained. It is a mere lovely creation of a romantic mind, and oftentimes, with such persons, fades away,

"And like the baseless fabric of a vision,
"Leaves not a rack behind."

It may be of service, therefore, to lay open the sources of domestic happiness, and to shew that these are to be found, not in the flowery regions of imagination, but in the sober realities of piety, chaste love, prudence, and well formed connexions. These precious springs are within the reach of all who will take the right path that leads to them: and this is the way of knowledge. We must make ourselves acquainted with the nature, designs, and importance of the family compact: we must analyse this union to ascertain its elements, its laws, and its purposes. Who can be a good member of any state, without knowing the nature of its constitution, and the laws by which it is directed? And it is equally vain to look for domestic happiness, without a clear insight into the ends and laws which Providence has laid down for the formation of the household.

In the discussion which have been agitated to settle the question as to the form of civil government best adapted to secure the welfare of the human race, the FAMILY CONSTITUTION has been too much overlooked. Speculation has been indulged, and theories proposed by their respective authors, in reference to the greater aggregations of society, with all the confidence of oracular authority; while at the same time, it is evident they have forgotten how much the well being of states is dependent on the well being of the families of which all states are composed. If there be any truth in the figure, by which a nation is compared to a pillar, we should recollect, that while individuals are the materials of which it is formed, it is the good condition of families that constitutes the cement which holds it together, and gives to it its fine form, solidity and durability. Let this be wanting, and however inherently excellent the materials, however elegant the shape, however ornamented the base, the shaft, or the capital may be, it contains in itself the principle of decay, an active cause of delapidation and ruin.

The domestic constitution is a divine institute. God formed it himself. " He taketh the solitary and setteth him in families; and like all the rest of his works, it is well and wisely done. It is, as a system of government, quite unique: neither below the heavens, nor above them, is there any thing precisely like it. In some respects it resembles the civil government of a state; in others, the ecclesiastical rule of a church; and it is there that the church and the state may be said to meet. "This meeting, however, is only on a very small scale, and under very peculiar circumstances." When directed as it should be, every family has a sacred character, inasmuch as the head of it acts the part of both the prophet and the priest of the household, by instructing them in the knowledge, and leading them in the worship of God; while at the same time, he discharges the duties of a king, by supporting a system of order, subordination and discipline. Conformably with its nature is its design : beyond the benefit of the individuals which compose it, and which is its first and immediate object, it is intended to promote the welfare of the national community to which it belongs, and of which it is a part : hence every nation has stamped a great value on the family compact, and guarded it with the most powerful sanctions. Well instructed, well ordered, and well governed families, are the springs, which, from their retirements, send forth the tributary streams that make up, by their confluence, the majestic flow of national greatness and prosperity : nor can any state be prosperous, where family order and subordination are generally neglected ; nor otherwise *than* prosperous, whatever be its political forms, where these are generally maintained. It is certainly under the wise instruction, and the impartial sceptre of a father, and within the little family circle, that the son becomes a good citizen ; it is by the fire side and upon the family hearth, that loyalty, and patriotism, and every public virtue grows ; as it is in disordered families, that factious demagogues, and turbulent rebels, and tyrannical oppressors, are trained up to be their neighbour's torment, or their country's scourge. It is there that the thorn and the brier, to use the elegant simile of the prophet, or the myrtle and the fir tree are reared, which are in future time to be the ornament and defence, or the deformity and misery of the land.

But, has the domestic constitution a reference only to the present world and its perishable interests? By no means. All God's arrangements for man, view him, and are chiefly intended for him, in his relation to eternity. The eye of Deity is upon that immortality to which he has destined the human race. Every family has in fact a sacred character belonging to it, which may indeed be forgotten or disdained; but the family is constituted, and ought, therefore, to be conducted with the prospect of the rising generation following that which precedes it, not only to the grave but to eternity."* Every member of every household is an immortal creature; every one that leaves the circle by death, goes into an eternity of torment or of bliss. Now since all the institutes of God look to another world as their chief and ultimate reference, surely, surely, that institute which is the most powerful of all in the formation of character, must be considered as set up with a special intention to prepare the subjects of it for " glory, honor, immortality, and eternal life."

No one judges aright of this household compact, nor can any be in a capacity rightly to perform its duties, who does not consider this double relation which it bears to the state and to the church, and who does not view it as a preparatory system, for training up the good citizen and the real christian. And for these objects, how great is the power which it really

---

* Anderson.

possesses: how considerable is the mutual influence of husbands and wives in moulding each others tastes, or modifying each others dispositions; of parents, in forming the character of their children and servants; and of brothers and sisters, in stimulating and guiding each others pursuits. The power of other constitutions is remote, occasional and feeble; but this is close, constant and mighty. With other systems the character is only casually brought into contact; but this always touches us. We live, and move, and have our being in the very centre of it. So powerful is the influence of this association on its members, that it has preserved them, by the blessing of God, in the possession of piety and morality, in times and places of the greatest corruption of manners. On what vantage ground does the conscientious christian parent here stand! The springs of public and social life may be greatly corrupted; the nation in which he dwells may degenerate into licentiousness, into idolatry, or into the most daring infidelity. Retiring then to this sacred enclosure, he may entrench himself, and there, lifting up a standard for God, either wait the approach of better days, or leave a few behind him, on whom the best blessings of those days will certainly descend. Though the heavens be shut up and there be no dew, the little enclosure which he cultivates, like the fleece of Gideon, will discover evident marks of the Divine favour. It actually seems as though in the wide scene, where the vices of the age may and can reign triumphant, this were some secure and sacred retreat, into which they cannot, dare not enter."*

It must be evident, however, that the great ends of the domestic economy, cannot be kept in view, nor the moral power of it displayed, unless the heads of it rightly understand their duty, and have a disposition properly to perform it. They must be christians in reality, or no christian government can be maintained. Where religion is wanting as the basis of their union, these happy fruits of it cannot be expected. The inferior and secondary object may be accomplished in the absence of parental piety, though neither so certainly, nor so effectually; but as to the more sublime and permanent end of the family constitution, which connects its members with the church of God on earth, and with the company of the redeemed in heaven, this cannot be looked for, where the father and the mother are destitute of true religion. Oh, how many interesting households are to be found, where all the mere social virtues are cultivated with assiduity, where the domestic charities all flourish, and public excellence is cherished, but which, on account of the want of vital godliness, are still losing the highest end of their union, are carrying on no preparatory course

* Mr. Anderson, in support and illustration of this beautiful sentiment, brings forward the families of the Kenites, and the Rechabites, whose history he traces, and shews it to be like a pure and vigorous stream, urging its course through a turbid lake, with the waters of which it refuses to blend, and maintaining its own characteristic, amidst surrounding impurity.

of education for the skies, and are destined to be swept away with the wreck of the nations that know not God, and with the wicked who shall be turned into hell. Alas, alas! that from such sweet scenes, such lovely retreats of connubial love and domestic peace, to which learning, science, wealth, elegance, have been admitted, religion should be excluded; and that while many wise and interesting guests are continually welcomed to the house, *He* only should be refused, who blessed the little family of Bethany; and who, wherever he goes, carries salvation in his train, and gives immortality to the joys which would otherwise perish for ever.

Precious, indeed, are the joys of a happy family; but, oh, how fleet! How soon, *must* the circle be broken up, how suddenly *may* it be! What scenes of delight, resembling gay visions of fairy bliss, have all been unexpectedly wrapt in shadow and gloom, by misfortune, by sickness, by death. The last enemy has entered the paradise, and by expelling one of its tenants, has embittered the scene to the rest; the ravages of death have been in some cases followed by the desolations of poverty, and they who once dwelt together in the happy enclosure, have been separated and scattered to meet no more. But religion, true religion, if it be possessed, will gather them together again, after this destruction of their earthly ties, and conduct them to another paradise, into which no calamity shall enter, and from which, no joy shall ever depart.

Happy then would it be, for all who stand related by these household ties, if the bonds of nature were hallowed and rendered permanent by those of divine grace. To found our union on any basis which does not contain religion in its formation, is to erect it on a quicksand, and to expose it to the fury of a thousand billows, each of which may overturn the fabric of our comfort in a moment: but to rest it upon religion, is to found it upon a rock, where we shall individually still find a refuge, when the nearest and the dearest relations are swept away by the tide of dissolution.

It is a pleasing reflection, that the domestic constitution depends not for its existence, its laws, its right administration, or its rich advantages, either upon family possessions, or the forms of national policy. It may live and flourish in all its tender charities, and all its sweet felicities, and all its moral power, in the cottage as well as in the mansion; under the shadow of liberty, and even under the scorching heat of tyranny. Like the church of which it is in some respects the emblem, it accommodates itself to every changing form of surrounding society, to every nation, and to every age. Forming with the church the only two institutions ever set up by God, as to their frame work; like its kindred institute, it remains amidst the ruins of the fall, the lapse of ages, and the changes of human affairs, the monument of what has been, the standing prediction of what shall be. Tyrants that crush the liberties of a state, cannot destroy the constitution of the family: and even persecutors that silence the preacher, and scatter the congregation, cannot hush the voice of parental instruction, or extinguish parental influence. Religion, hunted and driven by human power from the place of public concourse, would still find a retreat, as it often has done under such circumstances, in the household of faith; and *there* would keep alive, upon the family altar, that holy fire with which the sacrifices of the temple, under happier auspices, shall be offered. Neither families, nor the church of the redeemed, shall ever be entirely lost, whatever changes the world may yet have to pass through; "but blessing and being blest, will of themselves alone one day introduce the millenium."*

To all, therefore, who are united in the bonds of this relationship, I offer the consideration of these pages; which prescribe duties, and present advantages, belonging alike to all. Domestic happiness, in many respects, resembles the manna which was granted to the Israelites, in the wilderness; like that precious food, it is the gift of God which cometh down from heaven: it is not to be purchased with money; it is dispensed alike to the rich and to the poor, and accommodates itself to every taste; it is given with an abundance that meets the wants of all who desire it: to be obtained, it must be religiously sought in God's own way of bestowing it; and is granted to man as a refreshment during his pilgrimage, through this wilderness, to the celestial Canaan.

---

* See Anderson and Dwight.

CHAPTER II.

ON THE MUTUAL DUTIES OF HUSBANDS AND WIVES.

"See that ye love one another with a pure heart fervently."
ST. PETER.

MARRIAGE IS THE FOUNDATION OF THE DOMESTIC CONSTITUTION: this, says the Apostle, "is honourable in all;" and he has condemned, " as a doctrine of devils," the opinions of those by whom it is forbidden. It is an institute of God, it was established in Eden, was honoured by the personal attendance of Christ, and furnished an occasion for the first of that splendid series of miracles, by which he proved himself to be the Son of God, and the Saviour of the world. But there is another mark of distinction put upon it by the Holy Ghost, where it is said, "This is a great mystery, but I speak concerning Christ and the Church." Ephes. v. 32. Many commentators, I am aware, consider the term *mystery* as having no allusion to the nuptial tie, but as applying exclusively to the union of Christ and the church. If this be the case, it seems difficult to account for the introduction of this union at all, or to explain what bearing it has upon the subject in hand. Besides, the two-fold reference to the mediatorial undertaking of Christ, which is made by the apostle, when he enforces the duties of husband and wife, seems to confirm the opinion, that he represents the conjugal union, as a type or symbol of the close and endearing relation in which the church stands to its divine Redeemer. Nothing can throw a higher sanctity over this connexion, nor invest it with greater honour than such a view of it. Distinguishing, as it does, man from brutes; providing not only for the continuance, but for the comfort of our species; containing at once, the source of human happiness, and of all those virtuous emotions and generous sensibilities, which refine and adorn the character of man, it can never as a general subject be guarded with too much solicitous vigilance, nor be contracted, in particular instances, with too much prudence and care.

In proportion to the importance of the connexion itself, must be a right view and a due performance of the obligations arising out of it.

First. THERE ARE DUTIES COMMON TO BOTH PARTIES.

Secondly. THERE ARE DUTIES MORE PARTICULARLY ENJOINED UPON EACH.

My FIRST object will be to state those duties WHICH ARE COMMON TO BOTH HUSBAND AND WIFE.

1. The first which I mention, and which is the ground of all the rest, is LOVE.

Let this be wanting, and marriage is degraded at once into a brutal or a sordid compact. This duty which, though for reasons we shall consider in due place, is especially enjoined on the husband, belongs equally to the wife. It must be mutual, or there can be no happiness; none for the party which does *not* love, for how dreadful the idea of being chained for life to an individual for whom we have no affection; to be almost ever in the company of a person from whom we are driven back by revulsion, yet driven back upon a bond which prevents all separation and escape; nor can there be any happiness for the party that *does* love; such an unrequited affection must soon expire, or live only to consume that wretched heart in which it burns. A married couple without mutual regard, is one of the most pitiable spectacles on earth. They cannot, and, indeed, in ordinary circumstances, ought not to separate, and yet they remain united only to be a torment to each other. They serve one important purpose, however, in the history of mankind; and that is, to be a beacon to all who are yet disengaged, to warn them against the sin and folly of forming this union upon any other basis than that of a pure and mutual attachment; and to admonish all that are united, to watch with most assiduous vigilance, their mutual regard, that nothing be allowed to damp the sacred flame.

As the union should be formed on the basis of love, so should great care be taken, especially in the *early* stages of it, that nothing might arise to unsettle or loosen our attachments. Whatever knowledge we may obtain of each others tastes and habits before marriage, it is neither so accurate, so comprehensive, nor so impressive, as that which we acquire by living together; and it is of prodigious consequence, that when little defects are first noticed, and trivial faults and oppositions first occur, they should not be allowed to produce an unfavourable impression upon the mind. The remarks of Bishop Jeremy Taylor, in his inimitably beautiful sermon, entitled "The Marriage Ring," are so much in point, that I shall introduce a long extract in reference to this idea.

"Man and wife are equally concerned to avoid all offences of each other in the beginning of their conversation; every little thing can blast an infant blossom; and the breath of the south can shake the little rings of the vine, when first they begin to curl like the locks of a new weaned boy; but when by age and consolidation they stiffen into the hardness of a stem, and have by the warm rays of the sun, and the kisses of heaven, brought forth their clusters, they can endure the storms of the north, and the loud noises of a tempest, and yet never be broken: so are the early unions of an unfixed marriage; watchful and observant, jealous and busy, inquisitive and careful, and apt to take alarm at every unkind word. For infirmities do not manifest themselves in the first scenes, but in the succession of a long society; and it is not chance or weakness when it appears at first, but it is want of love or prudence, or it will be so expounded; and that which appears ill at first usually affrights the inexperienced man or woman, who makes unequal conjectures, and fancies mighty sorrows, by the proportions of the new and early unkindness. It is a very great passion, or a huge folly, or a certain want of love, that cannot preserve the colours and beauties of kindness, so long as public honesty requires a man to wear their sorrows for the death of a friend. *Plutarch* compares a new marriage to a vessel before the hoops are on; every thing dissolves its tender compaginations: but when the joints are stiffened and are tied by a firm compliance and proportioned bending, scarcely can it be dissolved without fire, or the violence of iron. After the hearts of the man and the wife are endeared and hardened by a mutual confidence and experience, longer than artifice and pretence can last, there are a great many remembrances, and some things present, that dash all little unkindnesses in pieces.

" Let man and wife be careful to stifle little things, that as fast as they spring, they be cut down and trod upon; for if they be suffered to grow by numbers, they make the spirit peevish, and the society troublesome, and the affections loose and uneasy, by an habitual aversation. Some men are more vexed with a fly than with a wound; and when the gnats disturb our sleep, and the reason is disquieted, but not perfectly awakened, it is often seen that he is fuller of trouble than if in the daylight of his reason he were to contest with a potent enemy. In the frequent little accidents of a family, a man's reason cannot always be awake; and when his discourses are imperfect, and a trifling trouble makes him yet more restless, he is soon betrayed to the violence of passion. It is certain that the man or woman are in a state of weakness and folly then, when they can be troubled with a trifling accident; and therefore it is not good to tempt their affections when they are in that state of danger. In this case, the caution is, to subtract fuel from the sudden flame; for stubble though it be quickly kindled, yet it is as soon extinguished, if it be not blown by a pertinacious breath, or fed with new materials. Add no new provocations to the accident, and do not inflame this, and peace will soon return, and the discontent will pass away soon, as the sparks from the collision of a flint: ever remembering that discontents proceeding from daily little things, do breed a secret undiscernible disease, which is more dangerous than a fever proceeding from a discerned notorious surfeit."

If they would preserve love, let them be sure to study most accurately each others tastes and distastes, and most anxiously abstain from whatever, even in the minutest things, they know to be contrary to them. The antients in their conjugal allegories, used to represent Mercury standing by Venus, to signify that by fair language, and sweet entreaties, the minds of each other should be united.

If they would preserve love, let them most carefully avoid all curious, and frequently repeated distinctions of MINE and THINE: for this hath caused all the laws, and all the suits, and all the wars in the world: let them who have but one person, have also but one interest. Instances may occur in which there may and must be, a separate investiture of property, and a sovereign independent right of disposal in the woman : in this case, the most anxious care should be taken by the husband, not to attempt to invade that right, and by the wife neither ostentatiously to speak of it, nor rigidly to claim it, nor selfishly to exercise it. In ordinary cases, " they should be heirs to each other, if they die childless; and if their be children, the wife should be with them a partner in the inheritance. But during their life the use and employment is common to both their necessities, and in this there is no other difference of right, but that the man hath the dispensation of all, and may keep it from his wife, just as the governor of a town may keep it from the right owner; he hath the *power*, but not the *right* to do so."

2. MUTUAL RESPECT is a duty of married life; for though, as we shall afterwards consider, especial reverence is due from the wife, yet is respect due from the husband also.

As it is difficult to respect those who are not entitled to it on any other ground than superior rank or common relationship, it is of immense consequence that we should present to each other that conduct which deserves respect and commands it. Moral esteem is one of the firmest supports and strongest guards of love : and a high degree of excellence cannot fail to produce such esteem. We are more accurately known to each other in this connexion, than either to the world, or even to our own servants and children. The privacies of such a relationship lay open our motives, and all the interior of our character; so that we are better known to each other than we are to ourselves. If therefore, we would be respected, we should be respectable. Charity covers a multitude of faults, it is true; but we must not presume too far upon the credulity and blindness of affection; there is a point beyond which even love cannot be blind to the crimson colouring of a guilty action. Every piece of real sinful conduct, the impropriety of which cannot be mistaken, tends to sink us in each others esteem, and thus to remove the safeguards of affection. Perhaps this has not been sufficiently thought of in wedded life, the parties of which have been sometimes anxious merely to cover their delinquencies from the world, forgetful that it is a dreadful thing to lose their mutual respect. It is delightfully striking to observe, how some pairs of eminent moral worth, regard each other; what reverence is blended with their love, and how like to angel forms of heavenly excellence they appear to one another.

In all the conduct of the conjugal state then, there should be the most marked and unvarying mutual respect even in little things: there must be no searching after faults, nor examining with microscopic scrutiny, such as cannot be concealed; no reproachful epithets; no rude contempt; no incivility; no cold neglect: there should be courtesy without ceremony; politeness without formality; attention without slavery; it should in short, be the tenderness of love, supported by esteem and guided by politeness. And then, we must maintain our mutual respectability before others: strangers, friends, servants, children, must all be taught to respect us from what they see in our own behaviour. It is in the highest degree improper, for either party to do an action, to say a word, or assume a look, that shall have the remotest tendency to lower the other in public esteem.

3. MUTUAL ATTACHMENT TO EACH OTHER'S SOCIETY, is a common duty of husband and wife.

We are united to be companions; to live together, to walk together, to talk together. The husband is commanded "to dwell with the wife according to knowledge." "This," says Mr. Jay, "intends nothing less than residence, opposed to absence and roving. It is absurd, for those who have no prospect of dwelling together, to enter this state: and those who are already in it, should not be unnecessarily abroad. Circumstances of various kinds will doubtless render occasional excursions unavoidable; but let a man return as soon as the design of his absence is accomplished, and let him always travel with the words of Solomon in his mind, 'As a bird that wandereth from her nest, so is a man that wandereth from his place.' Can a man while from home discharge the duties he owes to his household? Can he discipline his children? Can he maintain the worship of God in his family? I know it is the duty of the wife to lead the devotion in the absence of the husband; and she should take it up as a cross, if not for the time as a privilege. Few, however, are thus disposed, and hence one of the sanctuaries of God for weeks and months together is shut up. I am sorry to say that there are some husbands who seem fonder of any society than the company of their wives. It appears in the disposal of their leisure hours. How few of these are appropriated to the wife! The evenings are the most domestic periods of the day. To these the wife is peculiarly entitled—she is now most free from her numerous cares, and most at liberty to enjoy reading and conversation. It is a sad reflection upon a man when he is fond of spending his evenings abroad. It implies something bad, and it predicts something worse."

And to insure as far as possible the society of her husband, at his own fire side, let the wife be " a keeper at home," and do all in her power to render that fire side as attractive as good temper, neatness, and cheerful, affectionate conversation can make it; let her strive to make his own home the soft green on which his heart loves to repose in the sunshine of domestic enjoyment. We can easily imagine that even in Paradise, when man had no apparition of guilt, no visions of crime, no spectral voice from a troubled conscience, to make him dread solitude and flee from it, that even then, Adam liked not, on his return from the labour of dressing the garden, to find Eve absent from their bower, but wanted the smile of her countenance to light up his own, and the music of her voice to be the melody of his soul. Think, then, how much more in his fallen estate, with guilt upon his conscience, and care pressing upon his heart, does man now, on coming from the scenes of his anxious toil, need the aid of woman's companionship, to drive away the swarm of buzzing cares, that light upon the heart to sting it; to smooth the brow ruffled with sadness; to tranquillize the bosom agitated with passion; and at once to reprove and comfort the mind that has in some measure yielded to temptation. O woman! thou knowest the hour when the "good man of the house" will return at mid-day, while the sun is yet bowing down the labourer with the fierceness of his beams, or at evening, when the heat and burden of the day are past: do not let him, at such a time, when he is weary with exertion, and faint with discouragement, find, upon his coming to his habitation, that the foot which should hasten to meet him, is wandering at a distance; that the soft hand which should wipe away the sweat from his brow, is knocking at the door of other houses; nor let him find a wilderness, where he should enter a garden; confusion, where he ought to see order; or filth that disgusts, where he might hope to behold neatness that delights and attracts. If this be the case, who can wonder, that in the anguish of disappointment, and in the bitterness of a neglected and heart-stricken husband, he turns away from his own door, for that comfort which he wished to enjoy at home, and that society which he hoped to find in his wife, and puts up with the substitutes for both, which he finds in the houses of other men, or in the company of other women.

United to be associates then, let man and wife be as much in each other's society as possible; and there must be something wrong in domestic life, when they need the aid of balls, routes, plays, card parties, to relieve them from the tedium produced by home pursuits. I thank God, I am a stranger to that taste, which leads a man to flee from his own comfortable parlour and the society of his wife, from the instruction and recreation contained in a well stored library, or from the evening rural walk, when the business of the day is over, to scenes of public amusement, for enjoyment; to my judgment, the pleasures of home, and of home society, when home and home society are all that could be desired, are such as never cloy, and need no change, but from one kindred scene to another. I am sighing and longing, perhaps in vain, for a period when society shall be so elevated and so purified; when the love of knowledge will be so intense, and the habits of life will be so simple; when religion and morality will be so generally diffused, that men's homes will be the seat and circle of their pleasures; when in the society of an affectionate and intelligent wife, and of well educated children, each will find his greatest earthly delight; and when it will be felt to be no more necessary to happiness, to quit their own fire side, for the ball room, the concert, or the theatre, than it is to go from the well-spread table to the public feast, to satisfy the cravings of a healthy appetite: then will it be no longer imposed upon us to prove that public amusements are *improper*, for they will be found to be *unnecessary*.

But the pleasures of home must not be allowed to interfere with the calls and claims of public duty. Wives must not ask, and husbands must not give that time which is demanded for the cause of God and man. This is an age of active charity, and the great public institutions which are set up, cannot be kept in operation without great sacrifices of time and leisure by very many persons. Those who by their wisdom, talents, rank, or property, receive the confidence of the public, must stand prepared to fill up and conduct the executive departments of our societies; nor should they allow the soft allurements of their own houses, to draw them away from what is obviously the post of duty. We have known some, who, till they entered into wedded life, were the props and pillars of our institutions, yield so far to the solicitations of their new and dearest earthly friend, as to vacate their seat at the board of management for ever after. It is, I admit, a costly way of contributing to the cause of religion and humanity, to give those evening hours which could be spent so pleasantly in a country walk, or in the joint perusal of some interesting volume; but who can do good, or ought to wish to do it without sacrifices? I know an eminently holy and useful minister, who told the lady to whom he was about to be united, that one of the conditions of their marriage was, that she should never ask him for that time, which, on any occasion, he felt it to be his duty to give to God. And surely, any woman might feel herself more blessed in having sometimes to endure the loss of a husband's society, whose presence and talents are coveted by all public institutions, than in being left to the unmolested enjoyment of the company of one whose assistance is coveted by none.

4. MUTUAL FORBEARANCE is another duty.

This we owe to all, not excepting the stranger, or an enemy; and most certainly it must not be denied to our nearest friend. For the charity that " *suffereth long and is kind ; that envieth not ; vaunteth not itself, is not puffed up ; that doth not behave itself unseemly ; seeketh not her own ; is not easily provoked ; thinketh no evil ; rejoiceth not in iniquity, but rejoiceth in the truth ; that covereth all things ; believeth all things ; hopeth all things ; endureth all things :*" for this charity there is both need and room in every relation of life. Wherever sin or imperfection exists, there is scope for the forbearance of love. There is no perfection upon earth. Lovers, it is true, often fancy they have found it; but the more sober judgment of husbands and wives generally corrects the mistake; and first impressions of this kind, usually pass away with first love. We should all enter the married state, remembering that we are about to be united to a fallen creature : and as in every case, as Mr. Bolton remarks, it is not two angels that have met together, but two sinful children of Adam, from whom must be looked for much weakness and waywardness, we must make up our minds to some imperfection; and remembering that we have no small share of our own that calls for the forbearance of the other party, should exercise the patience that we ask. Where both have infirmities, and they are so constantly together, innumerable occasions will be furnished, if we are eager or even willing to avail ourselves of the opportunities for those contentions, which, if they do not produce a permanent suppression of love, lead to its temporary interruption. Many things we should connive at, others we should pass by with an unprovoked mind, and in all things most carefully avoid even what at first may seem to be an innocent disputation. Affection does not forbid but actually demands that we should mutually point out our faults; but this should be done in all the meekness of wisdom, united with all the tenderness of love, lest we only increase the evil we intend to remove, or substitute a greater one in its place. Justice, as well as wisdom, requires that in every case, we set the good qualities against the bad ones; and in most cases we shall find *some* redeeming excellencies, which, if they do not reconcile us to the failings we deplore, should at least teach us to bear them with patience; and the more we contemplate these better aspects of the character, the brighter will they appear: for it is an indubitable fact, that while faults diminish, virtues magnify in proportion as they are steadily contemplated. As to bitterness of language, and violence of conduct, this is so utterly disgraceful, and in the circle which I am accustomed to instruct, altogether so unusual, that it scarcely need be introduced even by way of cautioning against it. The ancients we are informed, took the gall from their nuptial sacrifices, and cast it behind the altar, to intimate the removal of all bitterness from the marriage state.

5. MUTUAL ASSISTANCE is the duty of husbands and wives.

This applies *to the cares of life.* Women are not usually very conversant with matters of trade, but still their counsel may be sought in a thousand cases with propriety and advantage. The husband should never undertake any thing of importance, without communicating the matter to his wife; who, on her part, instead of shrinking from the responsibility of a counsellor, and leaving him to struggle alone with his difficulties and perplexities, should invite him to communicate freely all his anxieties; for if she cannot counsel, she can comfort; if she cannot relieve his cares, she can help to bear them; if she cannot direct the course of his trade, she may the current of his feelings; if she cannot open any source of earthly wisdom, she can spread the matter before the Father and Fountain of Lights. Many men under the idea of delicacy to their wives, keep all their difficulties to themselves, which only prepares them to feel the stroke the heavier when it does come.

And then, as the wife should be willing to help the husband, in matters of business, *he* should be willing to share with her the burden of domestic anxieties and fatigue. Some go too far, and utterly degrade the female head of the family, by treating her as if her honesty or ability could not be trusted in the management of the domestic economy. They keep the money, and dole it out as if they were parting with their life's blood, grudging every shilling they dispense, and requiring an account as rigid as they would from a suspected servant: they take charge of every thing, give out every thing, interfere in every thing. This is to despoil a woman of her authority, to thrust her from her proper place, to insult and degrade her before her children and servants. Some, on the other hand, go to the opposite extreme, and take no share in any thing. My heart has ached to see the slavery of some devoted, hard working, and ill used wives; after labouring all day amidst the ceaseless toils of a young and numerous family, they have had to pass the hours of evening in solitude; while the husbands, instead of coming home to cheer them by their society, or to relieve them for only half an hour of their fatigue, have been either at a party or a sermon: and then have these hapless women had to wake and watch the live-long night, over a sick or restless babe, while the men whom they accepted as the partner of their sorrows, were sleeping by their side, unwilling to give a single hour of their slumber, though it was to allow a little repose to their toil-worn wives. Why, even the irrational creatures shame such men; for it is a well known fact, that the male bird takes his turn upon the nest during the season of incubation, to allow the female time to renew her strength by food and rest; and with her also, goes in diligent quest of food, and feeds the young ones when they cry. No man should think of marrying, who does not stand prepared to share, as far as he can do it with his wife, the burden of domestic cares.

They should be helpful to each other *in the concerns of personal religion.* This is clearly implied in the Apostle's language. " For what knowest thou, O wife, whether thou shalt save thy husband ? Or how knowest thou, O man, whether thou shalt save thy wife ?"* Where both parties are unconverted, or only one of them is yet a partaker of true piety, there should be the most anxious, judicious, and affectionate efforts for their salvation. How heathenish a state is it to enjoy together the comforts of marriage, and then travel in company to eternal perdition ; to be mutual comforters on earth, and then mutual tormentors in hell ; to be companions in felicity in time, and companions in torment through eternity! And where both parties are real christians, there should be the exercise of a constant reciprocal solicitude, watchfulness, and care, in reference to their spiritual and eternal welfare. One of the ends which every true believer should propose to himself, on entering the marriage state, is to secure one faithful friend, at least, who will be a helpmate for him in reference to another world, assist him in the great business of his soul's salvation, and that will pray for him and with him ; one that will affectionately tell him of his sins and his

---

* 1 Corinthians, vii. 16.

defects, viewed in the light of a Christian; one that will stimulate and draw him by the power of a holy example, and the sweet force of persuasive words; one that will warn him in temptation, comfort him in dejection, and in every way assist him in his pilgrimage to the skies. The highest end of the connubial state is lost, if it be not rendered helpful to our piety; and yet this end is too generally neglected, even by professors of religion. Do we converse with each other as we ought on the high themes of redemption by Christ, and eternal salvation? Do we study each other's dispositions, snares, troubles, decays in piety, that we may apply suitable remedies? Do we exhort one another daily, lest we should be hardened through the deceitfulness of sin? Do we practice fidelity without censoriousness; and administer praise without flattery? Do we invite one another to the most quickening and edifying means of grace of a public nature, and recommend the perusal of such instructive and improving books as we have found beneficial to ourselves? Do we mutually lay open the state of our minds on the subject of personal religion, and state our perplexities, our joys, our fears, our sorrows? Alas, alas! who must not blush at their neglects in these particulars? And yet such neglect is as criminal as it is common. Fleeing from the wrath to come, and yet not doing all we can to aid each other's escape! Contending side by side for the crown of glory, honour, immortality, and eternal life, and yet not doing all we can to ensure each other's success! Is this love? Is this the tenderness of connubial affection?

This mutual help should extend *to the maintenance of all the habits of domestic order, discipline, and piety.* The husband is to be the prophet, priest, and king of the family, to instruct their minds, to lead their devotions, and to govern their tempers; but in all that relates to these important objects, the wife is to be of one mind with him. They are in these matters, to be workers together, neither of them leaving the other to labour alone, much less opposing or thwarting what is done. "When the sun shines, the moon disappears; when he sets, she appears and shines; so when the husband is at home, he leads domestic worship, when he is absent, the wife must ever take his place." Some men refer the instruction of *young* children exclusively to their wives; and some wives, as soon as the children are too old to be taught upon the knee, think that they are exclusively the subjects of *paternal* care. This is a mistake in the important economy of the family, the members of which are never too young to be taught and disciplined by the father, nor to old to be admonished and warned by the mother; *he* may sometimes have a great influence in awing the rude spirits of the younger branches; while *her* soft persuasive accents may have delightful power to melt or break the hard and stubborn hearts of older ones. Thus they who have a joint interest in a family, must attend to them in the exercise of a joint labour.

They must be helpful to each other *in works of humanity and religious benevolence.*

Their mutual influence should be exerted, not in restraining, but in stimulating zeal, compassion, and liberality. What a beautiful picture of domestic life is drawn by the pen of the Old Testament historian. " And it fell on a day that Elisha passed to Shunem, where was a great woman; and she constrained him to eat bread. And so it was, that as oft as he passed by, he turned in thither to eat bread. And she said unto her husband, Behold now, I perceive that this is a holy man of God, which passeth by us continually. Let us make a little chamber on the wall, and let us set for him there a bed, and a table, and a stool, and a candlestick, and it shall be, that when he cometh to us, he shall turn in thither. And it fell on a day that he came thither, and he turned into the chamber, and lay there."* Every part of this scene is lovely. The generous and pious wish of the wife to provide accommodation for a destitute and dependent prophet; her prompt and prudent effort to interest her husband in the scheme of her benevolence: her discreet and modest keeping of her place in not acting without his permission; her dignified claim of a right to be associated with him in his work of mercy, for said she, let *us* make a little chamber on the wall: all is delightful, and as it should be, on her part: and no less so on the part of the man; for there was no surly

2 Kings, iv. 8, 11.

refusal, no proud rejection of the plan, because it did not originate with him, no covetous plea for setting it aside, on the ground of expense. Delighted, as every husband should be, to gratify the benevolent wishes, and support the liberal scheme of his wife, so far as prudence will allow, he consented; the little chamber was erected, and furnished by this holy pair, and soon occupied by the prophet; and never was a generous action more speedily or more richly rewarded. Elisha had no means of his own, by which to acknowledge the kindness; but He who said in after times, " he that receiveth a prophet in the name of a prophet, shall receive a prophet's reward," took upon himself, as he does in every instance, the cause of his necessitous servant, and most munificently repaid the generous deed.

A lovelier scene is not to be found on earth, than that of a pious couple, employing their mutual influence, and the hours of their retired companionship, in stirring up each other's hearts to deeds of mercy and religious benevolence; not Adam and Eve in Paradise, with the unspotted robes of their innocence about them, engaged in propping the vine, or trailing the rose of that holy garden, presented to the eyes of angels a more interesting spectacle than this. What a contrast does such a couple present, to the pairs which are almost every where to be found, whose calculations are not what they can save from unnecessary expense to bestow upon the cause of God and humanity, but what they can abstract or withhold from the claims of benevolence, to lavish upon splendid furniture, or domestic luxuries. Are there no wives who attempt to chill the ardour, to limit the beneficence, to stint the charities of their husband; who, by their incessant and querulous, and almost quarrelsome suggestions, that he is doing too much for others, and too little for his own family, drive the good man, notwithstanding he is lord of his own property, to exercise his liberality in secret, and bestow his charities by stealth? And what is oftentimes the object of such women? nothing more than the pride of ambition, or the folly of vanity. Only that they might have these parings of charity, to spend upon dress, furniture, and parties.

Perhaps the question will be asked, whether it is proper for a wife to give away the property of her husband in acts of humanity, or religious benevolence? Such an enquiry ought to be unnecessary; for no woman should be driven to the alternative of either doing nothing for the cause of God and man, or doing what she can by stealth. A sufficient sum ought to be placed at her disposal, to enable her to enjoy the luxury of doing good. Why should not she appear in her own name upon the honourable list of benefactors, and shine forth in her peculiar and separate glory, instead of being always lost in the radiance of *our* recorded mercy? Why should *she* have no sphere of benevolent effort? Why should *we* monopolize to ourselves the blessings of those that are ready to perish? It is degrading a married female to allow her no discretion in this matter, no liberty of distribution, no power to dispense, even in cases that concern her sex, but to compel her to beg first of a husband, *that* which others come to beg of her. If, however, she be unhappily united to a Nabal, a churl, whose sordid, grasping, covetous disposition, will yield nothing to the claims of humanity or religion, may she then make up for the deficiency of her husband, and diffuse his property unknown to him? I am strongly tempted to answer this question in the affirmative; for if in any instance we may deviate from the ordinary rule, and taking the man at his own word, which he uttered when in the solemn act of matrimony, he said, "with all my worldly goods I thee endow," may invest the wife with a joint proprietorship, and a right of appropriation, it is in such a case as this. But still, we must *not* sacrifice general principles to special cases; and therefore, I say to every female in such circumstances, obtain if you can, a separate and fixed allowance for charitable distribution; but if even *this* be not possible, obtain one for general personal expenses, and by a most rigid frugality, save *all* you can from dress and decoration, for the hallowed purpose of relieving the miseries of your fellow creatures.

6. MUTUAL SYMPATHY is required.

Sickness may call for this, and females seem both formed and inclined by nature to yield it.

> " O woman! in our hours of ease,
> Uncertain, coy, and hard to please,
> And variable as the shade
> By the light quivering aspen made;
> When pain and anguish ring the brow,
> A ministering angel thou!"

Unwilling, and indeed unable, to subscribe to the former part of this description, I do most readily assent to the truth of the latter. If we *could* do without her and be happy in health, what are we in sickness without her presence and her tender offices? Can we smooth, as woman can, the pillow on which the sick man lays his head? No. We cannot administer the medicine or the food as she can. There is a softness in her touch, a lightness in her step, a skill in her arrangements, a sympathy looking down upon us from her beaming eye, which ours wants. Many a female, by her devoted and kind attentions in a season of sickness, has drawn back to herself that cold and alienated heart, which neither her charms could hold, nor her claims recover. I entreat you, therefore, married females, to put forth all your power to sooth and please in the season of your husband's sickness. Let him see you willing to make any sacrifices of pleasure, ease, or sleep, to minister to his comfort. Let there be a tenderness in your manner, a wakeful attention and sympathy in your look, a something that seems to say, your only comfort in his affliction, is to employ yourselves in alleviating it. Hearken with patience and kindness to the tale of his lighter and even of his imaginary woes. A cold, heartless, awkward, unsympathising woman, is an exception from the general rule, and therefore a severer libel upon her sex.

Nor is this sympathy exclusively the duty of the wife; but belongs equally to the husband. He cannot, it is true, perform the same offices for her, which she can discharge for him: but much he can do, and all he can he *should* do. Her sicknesses are generally more numerous and heavy than his; she is likely, therefore, to make more frequent calls upon his tender interest and attention. Many of her ailments are the consequence of becoming his wife: she was, perhaps, in full vigour, till she become a mother, and from that time, never had a moment's perfect ease or strength again. That event which sent into his heart the joys of a parent, dismissed from her frame the comforts of health. And shall he look with discontent, and indifference, and insensibility, upon that delicate flower, which, before he transplanted it into *his* garden, glowed in beauty and in fragrance, to the admiration of every spectator? Shall he *now* cease to regard it with any pleasure, or sympathy, and seem as if he wished it gone, to make room for another, forgetting that it was *he* that sent the worm to the root, and caused its head to droop, and its colours to fade? Husbands, I call upon you for all the skill and tenderness of love, on behalf of your wives, if they are weak and sickly. Watch by their couch, talk with them, pray with them, wake with them: in all their afflictions, be you afflicted. Never listen heedlessly to their complaints: and oh, by all that is sacred in conjugal affection, I implore you, never, by your cold neglect, or petulant expressions, or discontented look, to call up in their imaginations, unusually sensitive at such a season, the phantom of a fear, that the disease which has destroyed their health, has done the same for your affection. Oh! spare their bosom the agonizing pangs of supposing that they are living to be a burden to your disappointed heart. The cruelty of that man wants a name, and I know of none sufficiently emphatic, who denies his sympathy to a suffering woman, whose only sin is a broken constitution, and whose calamity is the result of her marriage. Such a man does the work of a murderer, without his punishment, and in some instances, without his reproach; but not always without his design or his remorse.

But sympathy should be exercised by man and wife, not only in reference to their sicknesses, but to all their afflictions, whether personal or relative; all their sorrows should be common: like two strings in unison, the chord of grief should never be struck in the heart of one, without causing a corresponding vibration in the heart of the other; or, like the surface of the lake answering to the heaven, it should be impossible for calmness and sunshine to be upon one, while the other is agitated and cloudy: heart should answer to heart, and face to face.

Such are the duties common to both; the obligations peculiarly enjoined upon each, will be the subject of the next chapter.

CHAPTER III.

THE SPECIAL DUTIES OF HUSBANDS AND WIVES.

"Wives submit yourselves unto your own husband, as unto the Lord. For the husband is the head of the wife, even as Christ is the head of the Church: and he is the saviour of the body. Therefore as the church is subject unto Christ, so let the wives be to their husbands in every thing. Husbands, love your wives, even as Christ also loved the church, and gave himself for it; that he might sanctify and cleanse it with the washing of water by the word, that he might present it to himself a glorious church, not having spot, or wrinkle, or any such thing; but that it should be holy and without blemish. So ought men to love their wives as their own bodies. He that loveth his wife loveth himself. For no man ever yet hated his own flesh, but nourisheth and cherisheth it, even as the Lord the church: For we are members of his body, of his flesh, and of his bones. For this cause shall a man leave his father and mother, and shall be joined unto his wife, and they two shall be one flesh. This is a great mystery: but I speak concerning Christ and the church."
EPHESIANS v. 22—32.

OBSERVE the sublime and transcendently interesting fact which stands amidst the duties of domestic life, as stated by the apostle, in the language quoted above, like the sun in the centre of the planets, illuminating, impelling, and uniting them all. Every part of this most comprehensive and beautiful passage is inimitably striking. The design of the whole, is to magnify

Christ's love to the church; in order to this, the moral condition of the church, previous to the transforming work of redeeming grace, is supposed to be that of loathsome impurity; yet, notwithstanding this, he exercises the tenderest compassion for her welfare, and is not repelled by excessive defilement. To effect her redemption, he does not merely employ the operations of his power and of his wisdom, but surrendered himself into the hands of divine justice, that as a sacrifice of atonement, he might ransom the object of his regard at the price of his blood; thus manifesting an affection stronger than death, and "which many waters could not quench." The ultimate design of this act of mysterious humiliation, is to render her in some measure worthy of his regard, and meet for that indissoluble union with himself, into which, as his illustrious bride, she was about to be received. For this purpose, the efficient influences of the Holy Ghost were to be poured upon her mind, that in the cordial reception of the truth, she might be purified from iniquity, have the germ of every virtue implanted in her heart, and the robe of righteousness spread over her frame; till at length, under the dispensations of his providence, the means of his grace, and the sanctifying agency of his Spirit, the last spot of moral defilement might be effaced, the last wrinkle of spiritual decay removed, and like the "king's daughter, all glorious within, and with her clothing of wrought gold," she might be presented, covered with the beauties of holiness, to the Lord Jesus, in that day, "when he shall come to be admired in his saints, and glorified in all them that believe." Behold, what manner of love is this!! And it is *this* most amazing, this unparalleled act of mercy, that is employed by the apostle, as the motive of all christian conduct. He knew nothing of moral philosophy, if by this expression be meant, the abstract principles of ethics. He left as he found them, the grounds of moral obligations, but he did not enforce virtue by a mere reference to our relations to God as creatures, but by a reference to our relation to Christ as redeemed sinners. He fetched his motives to good works from the cross; he made the power of that to be felt, not only on the conscience as supplying the means of pardon, but upon the heart, as furnishing the most cogent, and at the same time the most insinuating argument for sanctification: he not only irradiates the gloom of despondency, or melts the stubborn obstinacy of unbelief, or stays the reckless progress of despair, by inspiring a feeling of hope, no; but by the death of a crucified Saviour, and an exhibition of his most unbounded compassion, he attacks the vice of the depraved heart, and inculcates all the virtues of the renewed mind. The doctrine of the cross is the substance of christian truth, and the great support of christian morals: and the apostle's mind and heart were full of it. Does he enforce humility? it is thus: " Let the mind be in you which was in Christ Jesus." An unreserved devotedness to God? it is thus: " Ye are not your own; for ye are bought with a price; therefore glorify God with your body and with your spirit, which are his." Brotherly love ? it is thus: " Herein is love, not that we loved God, but that he loved us, and sent his Son to be the propitiation for our sins. Beloved, if God so loved us, we ought also to love one another." A forgiving temper ? it is thus: " Be ye kind one to another, tender hearted, forgiving one another, even as God for Christ's sake hath forgiven you." Benevolence to the poor ? it is thus: " For ye know the grace of our Lord Jesus Christ, who, though he was rich, for our sakes became poor, that we, through his poverty might be made rich."* And who but an apostle would have thought of enforcing conjugal affection by a reference to the love of Christ to his Church ? And he has done this; and has thus represented redeeming love as a kind of holy atmosphere, surrounding the christian on all sides, accompanying him every where, sustaining the spiritual existence, the very element in which his religion lives, moves, and has its being. And this indeed, is religion: not a name, not a creed, not a form, not an abstract feeling, not an observance of times and places, not a mere mental costume, or holy dress which we put on exclusively for certain seasons and occasions: no ; but a moral habit, a mental taste, the spirit of the mind, which will spontaneously appear in our language, feeling, and behaviour, by a reference to Jesus Christ, as the ground of hope, and the model for imitation.

* Phil. ii. 5. 1 Cor. vi. 20. 1 John, iv. 10, 11. Ephes. iv. 32. 2 Cor. viii. 9.

In stating the duties especially enjoined on the two parties in the conjugal union, I shall begin with those of the HUSBAND. He is commanded to LOVE his wife.

As we have already shown, that this is a duty of both parties, the question very naturally arises, "For what reason is it so especially enjoined upon the husband? Why is *he* so particularly bound to the exercise of affection? Perhaps for the following reasons: 1. Because in the very nature of things *he* is most in danger of failing in his duty. Placed by the Creator as the " head of the wife," and invested with a certain right to govern his household, he is more in peril of merging the tender sensibilities in the predominant consciousness of superiority. 2. Because he is actually more deficient in this duty than the other party. This has ever been the case, in Pagan and Mahometan countries. In barbarous nations, especially, conjugal affection has ever been exceedingly weak, and it is probable, that even in the more civilized countries of Greece and Rome, it was not so generally strong and steady, as it has since been made by christianity. But without even going beyond the limits of Christendom, it may be truly said, that husbands are usually more deficient in love than wives: the latter, in my opinion, excel the former in tenderness, in strength, in constancy of affection. 3. Because a want of love on the part of the man, is likely to be attended with more misery to the other party: he can go to greater excesses in violence, in cruelty, in depravity. The want of this tender passion in *him* is likely to have a still worse effect upon his own character and the peace of the wife, than the want of it in her; in either case, a destitution of this kind, is a melancholy thing: but in him, it is on several accounts the most to be dreaded.

The apostle lays down two models or rules, for a husband's affection; the one is, *the love which Christ has manifested for his church;* and the other, *the love which a man bears for himself.*

In directing your attention to the first, I shall exhibit the properties of Christ's love, and show in what way *our* affection should be conformed to his.

Christ's love was SINCERE. He did not love in word only, but in deed, and in truth. In him there was no dissimulation; no epithets of endearment going forth out of feigned lips; no actions varnished over with a mere covering of love. *We* must be like him, and endeavour to maintain a principle of true regard in the heart, as well as a show of it in the conduct. It is a miserable thing to have to *act* the part of love, without feeling it. Hypocrisy is base in every thing; but next to religion, is most base in affection. Besides, how difficult is it to act the part well, to keep on the mask, and to support the character so as to escape detection! Oh, the misery of that woman's heart, who at length finds out to her cost, that what she had been accustomed to receive and value as the attentions of a lover, are but the tricks of a cunning dissembler.

The love of the Redeemer was ARDENT.

Let us, if we would form a correct idea of what should be the state of our hearts towards the woman of our choice, think of that affection which glowed in the breast of a Saviour, when he lived and died for his people. We can possess, it is true, neither the same kind, nor the same degree of regard, but surely when we are referred to such an instance, if not altogether as a model, yet as a motive, it does teach us, that no weak affection is due, or should be offered to the wife of our bosom. We are told by the Saviour himself, that if he laid down his life for us, it is our duty to lay down ours for the brethren; how much more for the "friend that sticketh closer than a brother." And if it be our duty *to lay down our life*, how much more to employ it while it lasts, in all the offices of an affection, strong, steady, and inventive. She that for our sake has forsaken the comfortable home, and the watchful care, and the warm embrace of her parents, has a right to expect in *our* regard, that which shall make her "forget her father's house," and cause her to feel that with respect to happiness, she is no loser by the exchange. Happy the woman, and such should every husband strive to make *his* wife, who can look back without a sigh upon the moment, when she quitted for ever, the guardians, the companions, and the scenes of her childhood?

The love of Christ to his church was SUPREME. He gives to the world his benevolence, but to the church his complacency. "The Lord thy God in the midst of thee," said the prophet, " is mighty; he will save thee, he will rejoice over thee with joy; he will rest in his love: he will joy over thee with singing." So must the husband regard his wife, above all else: he must "rest in his love." He should regard her not only above all *without* his house, but above all *within it.* She must take precedence both in his heart and conduct, not only of all strangers, but of all relatives, and also of all his children; he ought to love his children for her sake, rather than her for theirs. Is this always the case? On the contrary have we not often seen men, who appear to be far more interested in their children than in their wives; and who have paid far less attention to the latter than to grown-up daughters? How especially unseemly is it, for a man to be seen fonder of the society of any other woman, than that of his wife, even where nothing more may be intended than the pleasure of her company. Nor ought he to forsake her, in his leisure hours, for any companions of his *own* sex, however interesting might be their manners or their conversation.

The love of Christ is UNIFORM. Like himself, it is the same yesterday, to-day, and for ever. Conjugal affection should have the same character; it should be at all times, and in all places alike; *the same at home as abroad;* in other persons' houses as in our own. Has not many a wife to sigh and exclaim— "Oh! that I were treated in my own house, with the same tenderness and attention as I receive in company." With what almost loathing and disgust must such a woman turn from endearments, which under such circumstances she can consider as nothing but hypocrisy. Home is the chief place for fond and minute attention; and she who has not to complain of a want of it there, will seldom feel the need or the inclination to complain of a want of it abroad: except it be those silly women, who would degrade their husbands, by exacting not merely what is really kind, but what is actually ridiculous.

The love of the Redeemer was PRACTICAL and LABORIOUS. He provided every thing by his mediation for the welfare and comfort of the church, and at a cost and by exertions of which we can form no idea. It has been already declared that both parties are to assist in the cares of life. A *good* wife cannot be an idle one. Beautiful is her portraiture as drawn by the wise man. " Who can find a virtuous woman? for her price is far above rubies. The heart of her husband doth safely trust in her, so that he shall have no need of spoil. She will do him good and not evil all the days of her life. She layeth her hands to the spindle, and her hands hold the distaff. She stretcheth out her hand to the poor; yea she reacheth forth her hand to the needy. Her husband is known in the gates, when he sitteth amongst the elders of the land. She openeth her mouth with wisdom, and in her tongue is the law of kindness. She looketh well to the ways of her household, and eateth not the bread of idleness. Her children rise up and call her blessed: her husband also, and he praiseth her. Many daughters have done virtuously, but thou excellest them all. Favour is deceitful, and beauty is vain; but a woman that feareth the Lord, she shall be praised. Give her the fruit of her hands, and let her own works praise her in the gates." PROVERBS XXXI. This exquisite picture, combining as it does industry, prudence, dignity, meekness, wisdom and piety, cannot be too frequently or minutely studied, by those who would attain to high degrees of female excellence. The business of providing for the family, however belongs chiefly to the husband. It is yours my brethren to rise up early, to sit up late, to eat the bread of carefulness, and to drink if necessary, the waters of affliction, that you may earn by the sweat of your brow, a comfortable support for the domestic circle. This is probably what the apostle meant, when he enjoined us to give honour to the wife as to the weaker vessel: the honour of maintenance, which she in consequence of the weakness of her frame, and the frequent infirmities which the maternal relation brings upon her, is not so well able to procure for herself. In most barbarous countries, and in some half civilized ones, the burden of manual labour falls upon the female, while her tyrant lord lives in indolence, feeding upon the industry of the hapless being whom he calls a wife, but treats as a slave. And are there no such idle tyrants in our age and country, who so as they can live in indolence, and gratify their appetites, care not how they oppress their wives?— Wretches who do little or nothing for the support of the family? How utterly lost to every noble and generous sentiment must that man be whose heart cannot be moved by the entreaties or tears of an interesting woman, and who can hear in vain her pleadings for his child at her breast, and his child by her side, and who by such appeals cannot be induced to give up his daily visits to the tavern, or his habits of sauntering idleness, to attend to his neglected business, and stay the approaching tide of poverty and ruin. Such a creature is worse than a brute, he is a monster: and it seems a pity that there is no law and no convict ship to bear him away to a land where if he will not work, so neither could he eat.

In general, it is for the benefit of a family, that a married woman should devote her time and attention almost exclusively to the ways of her household: her place is in the centre of domestic cares. What is gained by *her* in the *shop*, is oftentimes lost in the house, for want of the judicious superintendence of a mother and a mistress. Comfort and order, as well as money, are domestic wealth; and can these be rationally expected in the absence of female arrangement? The children always want a mother's eye and hand, and should always have them. Let the husband, then, have the care of providing; the wife, that of distributing to the necessities of the family; for this is the rule both of reason and revelation.

And as Christ laboured for his church, not only during his abode upon earth, but made provision for its welfare when he departed from our world, in like manner should the husband take care of his wife. I never could understand the propriety of that custom, which is but too common, of men's providing by their wills so much better for the children than they do for the mother. Does this look like a *supreme* love? Every man who raises a woman to the rank of his wife, should take care, however inferior she might have been in circumstances before their marriage, to leave her in the situation into which he brought her: for it is indeed most cruel, to leave her to be deprived at once, not only of her dearest earthly friend, but of her usual means of comfortable subsistence.

A practical affection to a wife extends, however, to every thing; it should manifest itself in the most delicate attention to her comfort, and her feelings; in consulting her tastes; in concealing her failings; in never doing any thing to degrade her, but every thing to exalt her before her children and servants; in acknowledging her excellencies, and commending her efforts to please him; in meeting, and even in anticipating all her reasonable requests; in short, in doing all that ingenuity can invent for her substantial happiness and general comfort.

Christ's love to his church, was DURABLE and UNCHANGEABLE. " Having loved his own he loved them to the end," without abatement or alteration: so ought men to love their wives, not only at the beginning, but to the end of their union; when the charms of beauty have fled before the withering influence of disease; when the vigorous and sprightly frame has lost its elasticity, and the step has become slow and faltering: when the wrinkles of age have succeeded to the bloom of youth, and the whole person seems rather the monument, than the resemblance of what it once was. Has she not gained in mind what she has lost in exterior fascinations ? Have not her mental graces flourished amidst the ruins of personal charms ? If the rose and the lily have faded on the cheek, have not the fruits of righteousness grown in the soul ? If those blossoms have departed, on which the eye of youthful passion gazed with so much ardour, has it not been to give way to the ripe fruit of christian excellence ? The *woman* is not what she was, but the wife, the mother, the christian, are better than they were. For an example of conjugal love in all its power and excellence, point me not to the bride and bridegroom displaying during the first month of their union all the watchfulness and tenderness of affection, but let me look upon the husband and wife of fifty, whose love has been tried by the lapse and the changes of a quarter of a century, and who through this period and by these vicissitudes, have grown in attachment and esteem ; and whose affection, if not glowing with all the fervid heat of a midsummer's day, is still like the sunshine of an October noon, warm and beautiful, as reflected amidst autumnal tints.

But, before I go away from this view of a husband's especial duty, I must just advert to another rule of his regard which is laid down for him by the apostle. "So ought men to love their wives, *as their own bodies:* he that loveth his wife loveth himself." A man's children are parts of himself; his wife is himself: " for they two shall be one flesh." This is his duty and the measure of it too; which is so plain, that, if he understands how he treats himself, there needs nothing be added concerning his demeanour towards her; for "what mighty care does he take of his body, and uses it with a delicate tenderness, and cares for it in all contingencies, and watches to keep it from all evils, and studies to make for it fair provisions, and is very often led by its inclinations and desires, and does never contradict its appetites but when they are evil, and then also not without some trouble and sorrow." So let a man love his wife as his own body.

Can it be necessary to apply the force of *motives* to produce an appropriate attention to such a duty? If so, I appeal to your *sense of honour*. Husbands call to recollection the wakeful assiduities, and the tender attentions by which you won the affection and the confidence of the woman, who forsook her father and her mother, and the home of her childhood, to find a resting place for her heart in your attachment; and will ye falsify the vows ye plighted, and disappoint the hopes you raised? Is it accounted a disgraceful stigma on a man's reputation, to forfeit the pledges of a *lover?* oh! how much more dishonourable to forget those of a husband! That man *has* disgraced himself who furnishes just occasion to the partner of his days, to draw, with a sigh, a contrast between the affectionate attention she received as a lover and as a wife.

I urge affection to a wife by the recollection of *that solemn moment,* when in the presence of heaven and earth, before God's minister, and in God's house, you bound yourself by all the deeply awful formalities of a kind of oath, to throw open, and keep open your heart, as the fountain of her earthly happiness, and to devote your whole life to the promotion of her welfare.

I appeal to your regard to *justice.* You have sworn away yourself to her, and are no longer your own. You have no right to that individual, and separate, and independent kind of life, which would lead you to seek your happiness, in opposition to, or neglect of hers. " You twain are one flesh."

Humanity puts in its claim on behalf of your wife. It is in your power to do more for her happiness or misery, than any other being in the universe, but God himself. An unkind husband is a tormentor of the first class. His victim can never elude his grasp, nor go beyond the reach of his cruelty, till she is kindly released by the king of terrors, who, in this instance, becomes to her an angel of light, and conducts her to the grave as to a shelter from her oppressor. For such a woman there is no rest on earth: the destroyer of her peace has her ever in his power, for she is always in his presence, or in the fear of it; the circumstances of every place, and every day, furnish him with the occasions of cruel neglect or unkindness, and it might be fairly questioned, whether there is to be found on earth a case of greater misery, except it be that of a wretch tortured by remorse and despair, than a woman whose heart daily withers under the cold looks, the chilling words, and repulsive actions of a husband who loveth her not. Such a man is a murderer, though he escapes in this world the murderer's doom; and by a refinement of cruelty, he employs years in conducting his victim to her end, by the slow process of a lingering death.

If nothing else can prevail *interest* should, for no man can hate his wife, without hating himself, for " she is his own flesh." Love, like mercy, is a double blessing; and hatred, like cruelty, is a double torment. We cannot love a worthy object without rejoicing in the reflex beams of our own affection. Next to the supreme regard we cherish towards God, and which it is impossible to exercise and not hold communion with angels in the joys of heaven, connubial love is the most beatifying passion; and to transvenom *this* into unkindness is to open, at the very centre of our soul, a source of poison, which, before it exudes to torture others, torments ourselves.

I cannot here avoid inserting the exquisite and touching appeal, which Mr. Jay puts into the lips of married women to their husbands.—" Honour us; deal kindly with us. From many of the opportunities, and means by which you procure favourable notice, we are excluded. Doomed to the shades, few of the high places of the earth are open to us. Alternately we are adored and oppressed. From our slaves you become our tyrants. You feel our beauty, and avail yourselves of our weakness. You complain of our inferiority, but none of your behaviour bids us rise. Sensibility has given us a thousand feelings, which nature has kindly denied you. Always under restraints, we have little liberty of choice. Providence seems to have been more attentive to enable us to confer happiness, than to enjoy it.—Every condition has for us fresh mortifications; every relation new sorrows. We enter social bonds; it is a system of perpetual sacrifice. We cannot give life to others without hazarding our own. We have sufferings which you do not share, cannot share.—If spared, years and decays invade our charms, and much of the ardour produced by attraction departs with it.—We may die.—The grave covers us, and we are soon forgotten; soon are the days of your mourning ended; soon is our loss repaired; dismissed even from your speech, our name is to be heard no more—a successor may dislike it,—Our children, after having a mother by nature, may fall under the control of a mother by affinity, and be mortified by distinctions made between them and her *own* offspring.—Though the duties which we have discharged invariably, be the most important and necessary, they do not shine; they are too common to strike: they procure no celebrity; the wife, the mother fills no historic page. Our privations, our confinements, our wearisome days, our interrupted, our sleepless nights, the hours we have hung in anxious watchings over your sick and dying offspring."—But we forbear.

I NOW COME TO THE DUTIES ENJOINED UPON THE WIFE.

The first I mention is *subjection*.

" Wives submit yourselves unto your own husbands

as unto the Lord; for the husband is the head of the wife, even as Christ is the head of the church; and he is the saviour of the body. Therefore as the church is subject unto Christ, so let the wives be to their own husbands in every thing." The same thing is enjoined also in the epistle to the Colossians. Peter unites with Paul in the same strain. "Ye wives be in subjection to your own husbands." Before I state the *kind* of subjection here commanded, it is nesessary to state the nature of the authority to which it is to be yielded. Here I would observe, that with whatsoever kind and degree of authority the husband is invested over the wife, it is such *as is in no way incompatible with, nor trenches upon the strongest and tenderest affection.* And it is worthy of remark, " that the apostle does not enjoin husbands to rule, nor instruct them how, but merely to love; so that it seems to be with them, as with bishops and priests, to whom much honour is due, but yet so that if they stand upon it, and challenge it, they become less honourable."

It is such an authority, *as is compatible with religion* or the claims of God: for no man has a right to enjoin, and no woman is bound to obey, any command which is in opposition to the letter or spirit of the bible.—It is such an authority, *as is consonant with sound reason;* its injunctions must all be reasonable, for surely it is too much to expect, that a wife is to become the slave of folly, any more than of cruelty. It is an authority, *that accords with the idea of companionship.* It was very beautifully observed by an ancient writer, that when Adam endeavoured to shift the blame of his transgressions upon his wife, he did not say " the woman thou gavest *to* me," no such thing, she is none of his goods, none of his possessions, not to be reckoned amongst his servants; but he said " the woman thou gavest to be *with* me," that is to be my partner, the companion of my joys and sorrows.

Let conjugal authority be founded upon love, be never exercised in opposition to revelation or reason, and be regulated by the idea of companionship, and then there needs no particular rules for its guidance; for within such limits, it can never degenerate into tyranny; nor can it ever oppress its subjects: to such a power any woman may bow, without degradation, for its yoke is easy and its burden light. In every society, from that which finds its centre in the father's chair, to that which in a wider circle rests upon the throne, there must be precedence vested somewhere, and some ultimate authority, some last and highest tribunal established, from the decision of which there lies no appeal. In the domestic constitution this superiority vests in the husband: he is the head, the law-giver, the ruler. In all matters touching the little world in the house, he is to direct, not indeed without taking counsel with his wife, but in all discordancy of view, *he,* unless he choose to waive his right, is to decide; and to his decision the wife should yield, and yield with grace and cheerfulness. No man ought to resign his authority as the head of the family, no woman ought to wish him to do it: he may give up his predilections and yield to her wishes, but he must not abdicate the throne, nor resign his sceptre. Usurpation is always hateful, and it is one of the most offensive exhibitions of it, where the husband is degraded into a slave of the queen mother. Such a woman looks contemptible even upon the throne. I admit it is difficult for a sensible woman to submit to imbecility, but she should have considered this before she united herself to it: having committed one error, let her not fall into a second, but give the strongest proof of her good sense which circumstances will allow her to offer, by making that concession to superiority of station, which there is no opportunity in her case for her to do to superiority of mind. She may reason, she may persuade, she may solicit, but if ignorance cannot be convinced, nor obstinacy turned, nor kindness conciliated, she has no resource left but to—*submit:* and one of the finest scenes ever to be presented by the domestic economy, is that of a sensible woman employing her talents and address, not to subvert but to support the authority of a weak husband; a woman who prompts but does not command, who persuades, but does not dictate, who influences, but does not compel, and who, after taking pains to conceal her beneficent interference, submits to the authority which she has both supported and guided. An opposite line of conduct is most mischievous, for weakness, when placed in perpetual contrast with superior judgment, is rarely blind to its own defects; and as this consciousness of inferiority, when united with office, is always jealous, it is both watchful and recentful of any interference with its prerogative. There must be subjection then, and where it cannot be yielded to superior talents, because there are none, it must be conceded to superiority of station. But let husbands be cautious not to put the submission of their wives to too a severe a test. It is hard, very hard to obey a rash, indiscreet, and silly ruler. "If you will be the head, remember the head is not only the seat of government, but of knowledge. If you will have the management of the ship, see that a fool is not placed at the helm. Shall the blind offer themselves as guides?"

The grounds of submission are many and strong. Waving all motives founded upon the comparative strength of mind with which the two sexes may be gifted, I refer my female friends to less questionable matters. Look at the *creation;* woman was made *after* the man, "for Adam was first formed, then Eve." She was made *out* of man, "for the man is not of the woman, but the woman of the man." She was made *for* man, "neither was the man created for the woman, but the woman for the man." Look at the fall. Woman occasioned it. "Adam was not deceived, but the woman being deceived, was in the transgression." She was thus punished for it, "Thy desire shall be to thy husband, and he shall rule over thee." Look at her *history.* Have not the customs of all nations, antient and modern, savage and civilized, acknowledged her subordination? Look at *the light in which this subject is placed in the New Testament.* How strong is the language of the text, " the husband is the head of the wife, even as Christ is the head of the Church. Therefore as the church is subject unto Christ, so let the wives be to their own husbands in every thing."

Let me then, my respected female friends, as you would submit to the authority of Christ, as you would adorn the station that providence has called you to occupy, as you would promote your own peace, the comfort of your husband, and the welfare of your family, admonish you, meekly and gracefully to be subject in all things, not only to the wise and good, but to the foolish and ill-deserving. You may reason, as I have said before, you may expostulate, but you must not rebel or refuse. Let it be your glory to feel how much you can endure, rather than despise the institution of heaven, or violate those engagements into which you voluntarily and so solemnly entered. Let your submission be characterised by cheerfulness, and not by reluctant sullenness: let it not be preceded by a struggle, but yielded at once and for ever: let there be no holding out to the last extremity, and then a mere compulsory capitulation; but a voluntarily, cheerful, undisputed and unrevoked concession.

2. The next duty enjoined upon the wife is REVERENCE.

" Let the wife see that she reverence her husband." This duty is nearly allied to the last, but is still somewhat different. By reverence, the apostle means nothing of slavish, or obsequious homage. but that respect and deference which are due to one whom we are commanded to obey. Your reverence will be manifest in your *words:* for instance, in your manner of speaking *of* him, you will avoid all that will tend to lessen him in the esteem of others; all exposure of his faults or minor weaknesses; all depreciation of his understanding or domestic rule. Such gossip is detestable and mischievous, for can any thing tend more to irritate him, than to find that you have been sinking him in the esteem of the public? Reverence will be displayed in your manner of speaking *to* him. "Even as Sarah obeyed Abraham, calling him Lord:" all flippant pertness, every thing of contemptuous consciousness of superiority, of dictation and command, of unnecessary contradiction, of pertinacious and obtrusive disputation, of scolding accusation, of angry, reproachful complaint, of noisy and obstreperous expostulation, should be avoided. Almost all domestic quarrels begin in words; and it is usually in a woman's power to prevent them by causing the law of kindness to dwell upon her lips, and calming the gusts of her husband's passion, by those soft answers which turn away wrath. Especially should she be careful how she speaks to him, or even *before* him, in the company of her family, or of strangers: she must not talk him into silence; nor talk *at* him; nor say any thing that is calculated to wound or degrade him, for a sting inflicted in public is doubly charged with venom; she must not endeavour to eclipse him, to engross the attention of the company to herself, to reduce him to a cypher which is valueless till she stands before him. *This* is not reverence : on the contrary, she should do all in her power to sustain his respectability and dignity in public esteem, and her very mode of addressing him, partaking at once of the kindness of affection, and the deference of respect, is eminently calculated to do this. And should he at any time express himself in the language of reproof, even though that reproof be causeless, or unjustly severe, let her be cautious not to forget her station, so as to be betrayed into a railing recrimination, a contemptuous silence, or a moody sullenness. Difficult, I am aware it is, to shew reverence and respect, where there are no other grounds for it to rest upon than mere station; and as easy to pay it where wisdom, dignity, and piety, support the claims of relationship : but in proportion to the difficulty of a virtuous action, is its excellence ; and hers is indeed superior virtue, who yields, to the relationship of her husband, that reverence which he forbids her to pay to him on account of his conduct.

Her reverence will extend itself to her *actions,* and lead to an incessant desire to please him in all things. It is assumed by the apostle as an indisputable and general fact, that " the married woman careth how she may please her husband." All her conduct should be framed upon this principle, to give him contentment and to increase his delight in her. Let her appear contented with her lot, and that will do much to render him contented with his : while, on the other hand, nothing is more likely to generate discontent in *his* heart, than the appearance of it in her. Let her by cheerful good humour diffuse an air of pleasantness through his dwelling. Let her guard as much as possible against a gloomy and moody disposition, which causes her to move about with the silence and cloudiness of a spectre: for who likes to dwell in a haunted house? She should always welcome him across his threshold with a smile, and ever put forth all her ingenuity in studying to please him, by consulting his wishes, by surprising him occasionally with those unlooked for and ingenious devices of affection, which, though small in themselves, are the proofs of a mind intent upon the business of giving pleasure. The greater acts of reverent and respectful love, are often regarded as matters of course, and as such, produce little impression : but the lesser acts of attention which come not into the usual routine of conjugal duties, and into the every day offices which may be calculated upon with almost as much certainty as the coming of the hour which they are to occupy, these free-will offerings of an inventive and active affection, these extra tokens of respect, and expressions of regard, have a mighty power to attach a husband to his wife ; they are the cords of love, the bands of a man. In all her personal and domestic habits, her first care then, next to that of pleasing God, must be to please him, and thus hold to herself that heart, which cannot wander from her without carrying her happiness with it ; and which when once departed, cannot be restored by any power short of Omnipotence itself.

3. MEEKNESS is especially mentioned by the apostle Peter, as a disposition which it is the duty of every wife to cultivate.

He has distinguished and honoured this temper by calling it the *ornament* of a meek and quiet spirit. If there be some virtues, which seem pre-eminently to suit the female character, meekness bears a high place amongst such. No one stands in greater need of this disposition than the female head of a family: either the petulance and waywardness of children, or the neglects and misconduct of servants, or the sharp words of a husband, are almost sure, if she be easily provoked, to keep her in a state of irritation all the day long. How trying is a peevish woman, how odious a brawling one. " It is better to dwell in the wilderness than with a contentious and angry woman." The graces were females, says Mr. Jay, so were the furies too. It is astonishing the influence which meekness has sometimes had in a family: it has quenched the sparks and even coals of anger and strife, which but for this would have set the house on fire: it has mastered the tiger and the lion, and led them captive with the silken thread of love. The strength of woman lies not in resisting, but in yielding; her power is in her gentleness; there is more of real defence, aye and more of that aggressive operation too which disarms a foe, in one mild look, or one soft accent, than in hours of flashing glances, and of angry tones. When amidst domestic strife she has been enabled to keep her temper, the storm has been often scattered as it rose; or her meekness has served as a conductor to carry off its dreadful flashes, which otherwise would have destroyed the dwelling.

Put on then, the ornament of a meek and quiet spirit. Pay less attention to the decoration of the person, more to that of the mind. " Your adorning is not to be that outward adorning, of plaiting the hair, and of wearing of gold, or of putting on of apparel, but the hidden man of the heart, which is not corruptible." The language of another apostle on this subject is no less striking. " In like manner also, I will that women adorn themselves in *modest* apparel, with shamefacedness and sobriety; not with broidered hair, or gold, or pearls, or costly array : but which becometh women professing godliness, with good works." 1 Tim. ii. 9. 10. Two apostles, who both wrote as they were moved by the Holy Ghost, in such language as this, have denounced as improper, and as unbecoming a profession of godliness, a taste for immodest, expensive, or highly decorative dress.

Surely then, the subject is worthy the most serious attention of all christian females. By what sophistry can the letter, much more the spirit, of two passages of holy writ, so very plain and express in their terms as these, be set aside ? That they *are* set aside, is evident by the appearance of almost every congregation, into which we could enter on the sabbath day, whether within or without the Establishment. The race of folly, one should really suppose, is at length almost run, for it does seem well nigh impossible, even by the aid of our neighbours, the French, for the women of our age to render themselves more supremely ridiculous than many of them have lately appeared.* What with the gaudiness of colouring, and extravagance of form, our religious assemblies present every thing at once to disgust our taste, and to distress our piety.

> We have run
> Through every change that fancy at the loom,
> Exhausted, has had genius to supply;
> And studious of mutation still, discard
> A real elegance, a little us'd,
> For monstrous novelty and strange disguise.
> We sacrifice to dress, till household joys
> And comforts cease. Dress drains our cellar dry,
> And keeps our larder lean; puts out our fires;
> And introduces hunger, frost, and woe,
> Where peace and hospitality might reign.

It is high time for the christian teacher, to call back the women "professing godliness," from their wanderings in the regions of fashionable folly, to the Holy Scriptures: for the Holy Scriptures, it should be remembered, have laid down a general law for regulating the dress of the body, as well as that of the mind. I do hold then, that these passages of Scripture, are parts of revelation, and as such are still

---

* This is so notorious, that the inventors of caricatures, and the authors of newspaper satires, have made it the subject of their ridicule.

binding upon the conscience: if not, shew me when they were cancelled. I contend that *christian* females ought to abstain from expensive, showy, and extravagant fashions in dress, jewellery, and all kinds of unsuitable personal decoration. I am not arguing for a sectarian costume, for a religious uniform, for canonical shapes and colours, nothing of the sort, but for simplicity, neatness, economy; for, what the apostle calls, modest apparel, shamefacedness, and sobriety; for the *spirit* of the passages, if not the very *letter*; for a distinction between those who profess godliness, in their comparative inattention to such things, and those who make no such profession; for a proof that *their* minds are not so much engaged on these matters, as the minds of the people of the world are. I am not for extinguishing taste; alas, in matters of dress, this is already done; but for resisting the lawless dominion of folly, under the name of fashion. I am not for calling back the age of gothic barbarism, or vulgarity; no; I will leave ample room for the cultivation of both taste and genius, in every lawful department, but I am protesting against the desolating reign of vanity; I am resisting the entrance of frivolity into the church of God; I am contending against the glaring inconsistency of rendering our religious assemblies like the audience convened in a theatre. The evils of an improper attention to dress are great and numerous. 1. Much precious time is wasted in the study, and arrangements, and decisions of this matter. 2. The attention is taken off from the improvement of the mind and the heart, to the decoration of the person. 3. The mind is filled with pride and vanity, and a deteriorating influence is carried on upon what constitutes the true dignity of the soul. 4. The love of display infects the character. 5. Money is wasted which is wanted for relieving the misery, and improving the condition of mankind. 6. Examples are set to the lower classes, in whom the propensity is often mischievous in many ways.

I am aware it might be, and is said, that there may be the pride of singularity, as well as of fashion; the pride of being covered with sober autumnal tints, as well as of exhibiting the brilliant hues of the rainbow; the pride of quality and of texture, as well as of colour and of form. I know it, and I do not justify the one more than I do the other; I condemn all kinds: but at any rate there is a little more dignity in one kind than in another. I will leave opportunity for the distinctions of rank, for the inventions of true taste, and for the modest and unobtrusive displays of natural elegance and simple beauty; but I cannot allow the propriety of christian females yielding themselves to the guidance of fashion, however expensive, extravagant, or gaudy.

As to the employment of our artizans by the various changes of fashion, I have nothing to do with this, in face of an apostolic injunction. The silversmiths who made shrines for the worshippers of Diana might have pleaded the same objection against the preachers of the gospel, who certainly did, so far as they were successful, ruin this trade. I am only speaking to professors of religion, who form so small a portion of society, that *their* abstinence from folly would do but but little in diminishing the employment of the work people; and if it did, let them make it up in some other way. What I contend for, then, is not meanness, not ugliness, not unvarying sameness: no; but neatness opposed to gaudiness; simplicity and becomingness opposed to extravagance; modesty opposed to indelicacy; economy opposed to expensiveness. Whether what I contend for is characteristic of the age in which we live, let any spectator determine. I am anxious to see professors of religion displaying a seriousness and spirituality, a dignity and sobriety of mind, a simplicity of habits, and a sedateness of manners, becoming their high and holy profession; and all this, united with an economy in their personal expenses, which will leave them a greater fund at their disposal, for relieving the miseries and promoting the happiness of their fellow-creatures.

But, perhaps after all, many women may plead, that the gaity and expensiveness of their dress, is more to please their husbands than themselves: but even this must have its limits. And I really pity the folly of that man, who concerns himself in the arrangement of his wife's wardrobe and toilette; and who would rather see her go forth in all the gorgeousness of splendid apparel, to display herself in the drawing rooms of her friends, than in dignified neatness, to visit the cottages of the poor, as the messenger of mercy: and who rejoices more to contemplate her moving through the circles of fashion, the admiration of one sex, and the envy of the other, than to see her holding on her radiant course in the orbit of benevolence, clad in unexpensive simplicity, and with the savings of her personal expenditure, clothing the naked, feeding the hungry, healing the sick; and thus bringing upon herself the blessing of him that was ready to perish, and causing the widow's heart to sing for joy.

Let it be remembered, that not only the ornament, but the person which it adorns, is *corruptible*. Accidents may distort the finest form, diseases fade the loveliest colouring, time disfigure the smoothest surface, and death, the spoiler of beauty, work a change so awful and appalling, as to turn away the most impassioned admirers in disgust. How soon will every other dress be displaced by the shroud, and every other decoration be stripped off to make way for the flowers that are strewed in the coffin upon the corpse, as if to hide the deformity of death. But the graces of the heart, and the beauties of the character, are imperishable; such let a wife be continually seeking to put on; " for she that has a wise husband, must entice him to an eternal dearness, by the veil of modesty, and the robes of chastity, the ornaments of meekness, and the jewels of faith and charity; she must have no paint but blushings; her brightness must be her purity, and she must shine round about with sweetness and friendship, and then she shall be pleasant while she lives, and desired when she dies."

5. *Economy* and *Order* in the management of her personal and domestic expenditure, are the obvious duty of a wife.

You are to preside in the direction of household affairs; and much of the prosperity and comfort of the little community, will depend upon your skilful and prudent arrangements. There is a manifest disposition in this age, in all classes of society, to come as closely as possible to the habits of those above them. The poor are imitating the middling classes, and *they* are copying the upper ranks. A showy, luxurious, and expensive taste is almost universally cherished, and is displayed in innumerable instances, where there are no means to support it. A large house, a country residence, splendid furniture, a carriage, a retinue of servants, and large parties, are the aim of many, whose creditors pay for all. Christian families are in most imminent peril of worldly conformity in the present day; and the line of demarcation between the church and the world is fast wearing out. It is true they have no cards, they do not frequent the theatre, or the ball room, and *perhaps* they have no midnight routs;—but this is all: for many are as anxious about the splendour of their furniture, the fashion of their habits, the expensiveness of their entertainments, as the veriest worldling can be. Now a wife has great influence in checking or promoting all this. It has been thought that this increasing disposition for domestic show and gaiety, is to be attributed chiefly to female vanity. It is woman that is generally regarded as the presiding genius of such a scene : *she* receives the praise and the compliment of the whole, and *she* therefore, is under the strongest temptation to promote it. But let her consider, how little all this has to do with the happiness of the family, even in its most prosperous state ; and how a recollection of it aggravates the misery of adversity, when a reverse takes place. *Then* to be found in debt for finery of dress, or furniture ; *then* to have it said that *her* extravagance helped to ruin her husband ; *then* to want that, for bread, which was formerly wasted on luxury ; *then* to hear the whispered reproach of having injured others by her own thoughtless expenditure ! Avoid my female friends, these miseries; do not go on to prepare wormwood and gall to embitter still more the already bitter cup of adversity. Endeavour to acquire a skilfulness in domestic management, a frugality, a prudence, a love of order and neatness, a mid-way course between meanness and luxury, a suitableness to your station in life, to your christian profession ; an economy which shall leave you more to spare for the cause of God and the miseries of man. Rather check than stimulate the taste of your husband for expense; tell him that it is not necessary for *your* happiness, nor for the comfort of the family ; draw him away from these adventitious circumstances, to the mental improvement, the moral culture, the religious instruction, of your children. Let knowledge, piety, good sense, well-formed habits, harmony, mutual love, be the sources of your domestic pleasures : what is splendour of furniture, or dress, or entertainments, to these ?

6. A wife SHOULD BE MOST ATTENTIVE TO ALL THAT CONCERNS THE WELFARE AND COMFORT OF THE CHILDREN, if there be any.

For this purpose, she must be *a keeper at home*.— " That they may teach the young wives to be sober, to love their husbands, to love their children, to be discreet, chaste, *keepers at home*." And how can the duties that devolve upon the female head of a family be well discharged, if she be not a keeper at home ?— On this I have dwelt already in a former chapter, but its importance will justify my returning to the subject again. How much has she to attend to, how many cares to sustain, how many activities to support, where there is a young family ? Whoever has leisure for gossiping, *she* has none : whoever may be found wandering from house to house, " hearing or telling some new thing," *she* must not. A mother's place is in the midst of her family; a mother's duties are to take care of *them*. Nothing can excuse a neglect of these; and yet we often see such neglect. Some are *literary characters*, and the welfare of the household is neglected for books. Not that I would debar a female from the luxury of reading, or sink her to a mere domestic drudge, whose ceaseless toils must have no intermission nor solace from literature ; far from it: but her taste for literature must be kept within due bounds, and not be allowed to interfere with her household duties. No husband can be pleased to see a book in the hands of a wife, while the house is in confusion, and the children's comfort unprovided for. Much less should *a taste for company* be allowed to draw a wife too much out of the circle of her care and duties. To be wandering from house to house in the morning, or to be engaged till a late hour evening after evening, at a party, while the family at home are left to themselves, or to the care of servants, is certainly disgraceful. Even attention to the *public* duties of *religion* must be regulated by a due regard to domestic claims. I am aware that many are apt to make these claims an excuse for neglecting the public means of grace almost entirely: the house of God is unfrequented: sermons, sacramental seasons, and all other religious meetings, are given up, for an absorbing attention to household affairs. This is one extreme; and the other is, such a devotedness to religious meetings, that the wants of a sick family, the cries of a hungry infant, or the circumstances of some extraordinary case of family care, are not allowed to have any force in detaining a mother from a week-day sermon, a prayer meeting, or the anniversary of some public institution. It is no honour to religion for a wife, under such circumstances, to be seen in the house of God; duties cannot be in opposition to each other; and at such a time, her's lie at home. It must be always distressing, and in some cases disgusting, for a husband, on his returning to a scene of domestic confusion, and seeing a neglected child in the cot, to be told, upon enquiring after the mother, that she is attending a sermon or public meeting. There is great need for watchfulness in the present age, when female agency is in such requisition, lest attention to public institutions should most injuriously interfere with the duties of a wife and a mother. I know very well that an active woman, may by habits of order, punctuality, and despatch, so arrange her more direct and immediate duties at home, as to allow of sufficient leisure to assist the noble societies which solicit her patronage, without neglecting her husband and children: but where this cannot be done, no society, whether humane or religious, should be allowed to take her away from what is after all, her first and more appropriate sphere. She *must* be *a keeper at home,* if any thing there demands her presence.

Such appear to me to be the leading duties of a wife. Motives of a very high and sacred character may be offered for a diligent performance of them. *Her own comfort,* and that of her husband, is of course most vitally connected with a fulfilment of her obligations: and the welfare of her children is also deeply involved. And then, her character shines forth with peculiar lustre. A GOOD WIFE is a high attainment in female excellence: it is woman in her brightest glory since the fall. But there is one consideration of supreme importance mentioned by the apostle, to which I shall direct your attention.—" Likewise ye wives, be in subjection to your own husbands, that if any obey not the word, they also may without the word be won by the conversation of the wives, while they behold your chaste conversation, coupled with fear." Powerful and yet tender consideration! Mark, my female friends, the implied eulogy passed by the apostle on *your* sex, where he seems to take it for granted, that if one party be destitute of religion, it is the husband. And facts prove that this assumption was correct. Religion flourishes most among the female part of our species : in our congregations, and in our churches, the greater number is of *them*. Can we account for this by natural causes ? Partly. They are more at home, and therefore more within the means of grace :—they are more susceptible;—they are less exposed to those temptations that harden the heart through the deceitfulness of sin ; they are subject to more affliction, which *softens* the heart and prepares it for the seed of the kingdom ;—but all this is not enough, for without grace all these advantages are unavailing : we must resolve it therefore into divine purpose, divine interposition, and the arrangements of divine wisdom. Female influence in all civilized states is great ; and God has generally made much use of this wherever the gospel has come, as one of the means for spreading religion. He pours his grace on *them*, that their influence may be employed with others, especially their husbands and their children. If then, in any case, a christian woman be united to an unconverted man, she must cherish and display a deep, and tender, and judicious solicitude for his salvation : and " what knowest thou, O wife, whether thou shalt save thy husband." I would not encourage unequal marriages : I would not have the single try the doubtful and dangerous experiment of marrying an irreligious man, in the hope of converting him; in such cases the conversion is often the other way; but where the union *is* formed, there I say, nourish the anxiety, and employ every discreet exertion for his eternal welfare. Many instances have occurred, in which the unbelieving husband has been sanctified by the wife. She has drawn him with the cords of a tender and judicious love, to a consideration of the subject of personal religion. Think of the value of a soul, and of the ineffable glory of being the instrument of its salvation. But O! to be the means of saving the soul of a husband! Think how it will strengthen the bond, and sanctify and sweeten it, which unites you on earth and in time; and at the same time add to it a tie, by which you shall "not lose one another in the valley of the shadow of death," but be reunited as kindred spirits, though not as man and wife, in heaven, and through eternity. "Think, O wife, of the happiness—the honour that awaits you. What is the triumph you have acquired over him by your charms, compared with the victory you will obtain over him by your religion?—What pleasure will attend you the remainder of your days—now you are of 'one heart and one mind;' now you 'take sweet counsel together.' The privileged language of prayer now is —' OUR Father :—of every motion made to go and seek the Lord of Hosts there is a ready acceptance— 'I will go also.' And what will be your joy and crown of rejoicing in that day, when before assembled men and angels, he will say, O blessed be the Providence which attached us in yonder world and has still more perfectly united us in this. The woman thou gavest to be with me, led me not to the tree of knowledge of good and evil, but to the tree of life which is in the midst of the Paradise of God."*

But how is this solicitude to be employed? The apostle tells us: " that they may be won by the conversation of their wives, while they BEHOLD your chaste conversation, coupled with fear." Your religion must be seen embodied in your whole character and conduct. It must commend itself to their judgment by what they perceive, as sincere. It must be *consistent;* for a want of uniformity, however earnest it may in many respects and at many times appear, will produce disgust. You must " let your light so shine before them, that they *seeing* your good works, may glorify God." You must ever appear invested with all the beauty of a lovely example, which, silent though you be as it respects your tongue, is living eloquence. Your religion must diffuse its lustre over your whole character, and impress itself most deeply on your relation as a wife, and a mother; it must be a new motive to all that respect, and reverence, and devotedness, and meekness, which have been laid before you, and it must lead you to carry every conjugal and maternal virtue to the highest degree of perfection. It must be attended with the most profound humility, for if there be any spiritual pride, any conscious and

* Mr. Jay.

manifest sense of superiority, any thing approaching to the pharisaic temper, which says, " stand by, I am holier than thou," any thing like contempt of your husband, as an unconverted sinner, you will excite an inveterate prejudice not only against religion, but against yourself; religion will be hated by him for your sake, and you for religion's sake. When you venture to speak to him on the subject of piety, it should be as remotely as possible from all lecturing, all dictation, all reproach, all conscious superiority; and with all possible tenderness, meekness, humility, and persuasive affection. Never talk to him of his state *before others*, and never talk *at* him. Nor is it likely to accomplish the object you have in view, to weary him by continual importunity. Many defeat their own end, by an incessant introduction of the subject, and sometimes with an asperity which increases the revulsion, which its own nature is calculated, in such a mind to produce. An occasional hint, and that of the most tender, respectful, and delicate kind, is all that you should attempt, and then leave your example to speak. Occasionally you may put an instructive volume in his way, and solicit his perusal of it. Do not bring your religious friends too much about you, so as to annoy him: especially keep away as much as possible, any that may have a less portion of discretion than the rest; and confine yourself to the more judicious, and best informed. Never rudely interfere with his pursuits, his reading, or his company, although they may not be what *you* can cordially approve. Till he is enlightened from above, he will not see the evil of these things, and to attempt to interrupt him, in any other way, than by the mildest, and most respectful expostulation, will only do harm. Should he wish to draw you from the high pursuit of eternal life, you are not, of course, in this case, to yield to his persuasion, nor in any thing to concede, where your conscience is decidedly concerned in the matter. You must be firm, but mild. One concession granted by you, would only lead to another. But still, even in this extremity, your resistance of his attempts to interfere with your religion, must be maintained in all the meekness of religion, and must be attended with fresh efforts to please, in all things which are lawful. If such a line of conduct should subject you to reproach, anger, and persecution, a most painful, and by no means an uncommon case, you must possess your soul in patience, and commit your way to Him, that judgeth righteously. Many a persecuting husband has been subdued, if not to religion, yet to kinder conduct, by the meek and uncomplaining temper of his wife.

To conclude. Let us all seek after more of the spirit of true religion,—the spirit of faith, of hope, of prayer: a faith, that really believes the word of God, and looketh habitually to the cross of Christ by which we obtain salvation, and to the eternal world where we shall fully and for ever enjoy it: a hope that lives in the expectation and desire of glory, honour, immortality, and eternal life: and a spirit of prayer which leads us daily and hourly to the throne of divine grace, for all that aid of the Holy Ghost, which we need, not only for the duties that refer to our relations to another world, but for those which devolve upon us, in consequence of our relations in this. "Godliness is profitable for all things, having the promise of the life that now is, as well as of that which is to come." The same principle of divine grace which unites us to God, will bind us closer to each other. Religion contains in it not only the seeds of immortal virtues, but of such as are mortal: not only the germs of excellences which are to flourish in the temple of heaven, but which grow up in the house of our pilgrimage upon earth, to enliven with their beauty, and to refresh with their fragrance, the domestic circle. A good christian cannot be a bad husband, or father; and other things being equal, he who has most piety, will shine most in all the relations of life. A bible placed between man and wife as the basis of their union, the rule of their conduct, and the model of their spirit, will make up many a difference, comfort them under many a cross, guide them in many a strait, wherein flesh and blood will be confounded and at a loss, support them in their last sad parting from each other, and re-unite them in the world where they shall go no more out.

"Those married pairs that live, as remembering that they must part again, and give an account how they treat themselves and each other, shall at the day of their death, be admitted to glorious espousals; and when they shall live again, be married to their Lord, and partake of his glories. All those things that now please us, shall pass from us, or we from them: but those things that concern the other life, are permanent as the numbers of eternity: and although at the resurrection, there shall be no relation of husband and wife, and no marriage shall be celebrated but the marriage of the Lamb, yet then shall be remembered how men and women passed through this state, which is a type of that; and from this sacramental union, all holy pairs shall pass to the spiritual and eternal, where love shall be their portion, and joys shall crown their heads, and they shall lie in the bosom of Jesus, and in the heart of God to eternal ages." Amen.

CHAPTER IV.

SOME REMARKS ON THE FORMATION OF THE MARRIAGE UNION.

"Methinks it is a misfortune that the marriage state, which in its own nature is adapted to give us the completest happiness this life is capable of, should be so uncomfortable a one to so many as it daily proves. But the mischief generally proceeds from the unwise choice people make for themselves, and an expectation of happiness from things incapable of giving it. Nothing but the good qualities of the person beloved, can be a foundation for a love of judgment and discretion; and whoever expects happiness from any thing but virtue, wisdom, good humour, and a similitude of manners, will find themselves widely mistaken."

SPECTATOR.

THE preceding chapters make it evident, that marriage is a step of incalculable importance, and ought never to be taken without the greatest consideration and the utmost caution. If the duties of this state are so numerous and so weighty, and if the right discharge of these obligations, as well as the happiness of our whole life, and even our safety for eternity, depend, as they necessarily must do, in no small measure upon the choice we make of a husband or wife, then let reason determine, with what deliberation we should advance to such a connexion. It is obvious, that no decision of our whole earthly existence requires more of the exercise of a calm judgment than this, and yet observation proves how rarely the judgment is allowed to give counsel, and how generally the imagination and the passions settle the business. A very great portion of the misery and of the crime with which society is depraved and afflicted, is the result of ill-formed marriages. If mere passion without prudence, or covetousness without love, be allowed to guide the choice, no wonder that it is improperly done, or that it is highly disastrous in its consequences; and how often are passion and covetousness alone consulted. To use the beautiful language quoted by me in another work, where I have treated briefly the subject of this chapter, I would remark, "that they who enter the marriage state, cast a die of the greatest contingency, and yet of the greatest interest in the world, next to the last throw for eternity. Life or death, felicity or a lasting sorrow, are in the power of marriage. A woman indeed ventures most, for she hath no sanctuary to retire to, from an evil husband; she must dwell upon her sorrow, which her own folly hath produced; and she is more under it, because her tormentor hath warrant of prerogative, and the woman may complain to God, as subjects do of tyrant princes, but otherwise she hath no appeal in the causes of unkindness. And though THE MAN can run from many hours of sadness, yet he must return to it again; and when he sits among his neighbours, he remembers the objection that lies in his bosom, and he sighs deeply." If however, it were merely the comfort of the married pair themselves that was concerned, it would be a matter of less consequence, a stake of less value; but the well-being of a family, not only for this world, but for the next, and equally so the well-being of *their* descendants, even to a remote period, depends upon this union. In the ardour of passion, few are disposed to listen to the counsels of prudence; and perhaps there is no advice, generally speaking, more thrown away, than that which is offered on the subject of marriage. Most persons, especially if they are already attached to a selected object, although they have not committed themselves by a promise or even a declaration, will go on in the pursuit, blinded by love to the indiscretion of their choice; or desperately determined, with the knowledge of that indiscretion, to accomplish if possible, their purpose. Upon such individuals, reasoning is wasted, and they must be left to gain wisdom in the only way, by which some will acquire it, painful experience. To others who may be yet disengaged, and disposed to hearken to the language of advice, the following remarks are offered.—

In the affair of marriage, BE GUIDED BY THE ADVICE OF PARENTS OR GUARDIANS. Parents have no right to *select* for you, nor ought you to select for yourself, without consulting with them. How far they are vested with authority to prohibit you from marrying a person whom they disapprove, is a point of casuistry, very difficult to determine. If you are of age, and able to provide for yourselves, or are likely to be well provided for by those to whom you are about to be united, it is a question whether they can do any thing more than advise and persuade; but *till you are of age*, they have positive authority to *forbid;* and it is an undutiful act in you, to form connexions without their knowledge, and to carry them on against their prohibitions. Their objections ought always, I admit, to be founded on reason, and not on caprice, pride, or cupidity: for where this is the case, and children are of full age, and are guided in their choice by prudence, by piety, and by affection, they certainly may, and must be left to decide for themselves. Where, however, parents rest their objections on sufficient grounds, and shew plain and palpable reasons for prohibiting a connexion, there it is the manifest duty of sons, and especially of daughters, to give it up. A union formed in opposition to the reasonable objection of a discreet father or mother is very rarely a happy one; and the bitter cup is rendered additionally bitter, in such a case, by the wormwood and gall of self reproach. What miseries of this kind have we all seen! How many beacons are set up, if young people would but look at them, to warn them against the folly of giving themselves up to the impulse of an imprudent attachment, and following it to a close, against the advice, remonstrance, and prohibition of their parents. Very seldom does that connexion prove otherwise than a source of wretchedness, on which the frown of an affectionate and wise father and mother fell from the beginning; for God seems to rise up in judgment, and to support the parent's authority, by confirming their displeasure with his own.

Marriage should in every case be formed UPON THE BASIS OF MUTUAL ATTACHMENT. If there be no love *before* marriage, it cannot be expected there should be any after it. Lovers, as all are supposed to be who are looking forward to this union, without love, have no right to expect happiness; the coldness of indifference is soon likely, in their case, to be changed into aversion. There ought to be *personal* attachment. If there be any thing, even in the exterior, that excites disgust, the banns are forbidden by the voice of nature. I do not say that beauty of countenance, or elegance of form is necessary; by no means; a pure and strong attachment has often existed in the absence of these; and I will not take upon me to determine that it is absolutely *impossible* to love *deformity*, but we certainly ought not to unite ourselves with it, unless we *can* love it; or at least, are so enamoured with the fascination of mental qualities that may be united with it, as to lose sight of the body in the charms of the mind, the heart, and the manners. All I contend for, is, that to proceed to marriage against absolute dislike and revulsion, is irrational, base, and sinful.

But love should respect the mind, as well as the body; for to be attached to an individual simply on the ground of beauty, is to fall in love with a doll, or a statue, or a picture; such an attachment is lust or fancy, but certainly not a rational affection. If we love the body, but do not love the mind, the heart, and the manners, our regard is placed upon the inferior part of the person, and therefore, only upon that which by disease may be next year a very different thing to what it is now. Nothing fades so soon as beauty; it is but like the delicate bloom of an attractive fruit, and if there be nothing agreeable underneath, will be thrown away in disgust when that is brushed off; and thrown away, too, by the very hand of him that plucks it. It is so commonly remarked, as to be proverbial, that the charms of mind increase by acquaintance, while those of the exterior diminish; and that while the former easily reconciles us to a plain countenance, the latter excite, by the power of contrast, a distaste for the insipidity, ignorance, and heartlessness, with which they are united, like gaudy, scentless flowers, growing in a desert. Instead of determining to stake our happiness upon the act of gathering these blooming weeds, to place them in our bosom, let us ask how they will look a few years hence, or how they will adorn and bless our habitation? Let us ask, will the understanding, united with that countenance, render its subject fit to be my companion, and the instructor of my children? Will that temper patiently bear with my weaknesses, kindly consult my tastes, affectionately study my comfort? Will those manners please me in solitude, as well as in society? Will those habits render my dwelling pleasant to myself and to my friends? We must try *these* matters, and hold our passions back, that we may take counsel with our judgment, and suffer reason to come down and talk with us in the cool of the evening.

Such then, is the love on which marriage should be contracted,—love to the whole person; love to the mind, and heart, and manners, as well as to the countenance and form; love tempered with respect; for this only is the attachment that is likely to survive the charms of novelty, the spoliation of disease, and the influence of time: that is likely to support the tender sympathies and exquisite sensibilities of the conjugal state; and render man and wife to the verge of extreme old age, what it was the intention of him who instituted the marriage union they should be,—the help and the comfort of each other.

By what language then, sufficiently strong and indignant, can we reprobate those compacts, so disgraceful, and yet so common, by which marriage is converted into *a money speculation, a trading enterprise, a mere business of pounds, shillings, and pence?* How cruel a part do those parents act, who for the sake of an advantageous settlement, urge their daughters into a union, from which their hearts revolt; or persuade their sons to marry women, towards whom they feel no affection, merely for the sake of a fortune! Unnatural fathers and mothers! is it thus ye would lead your children, decorated as sacrifices to the shrine of Mammon, and act the part of priests and priestesses *yourselves*, in the immolation of these hapless victims!! What will *you* assist in the rites of this legal prostitution? Can none others be found but *you*, the natural guardians of your children's interests, to persuade them to sell their persons, and barter all the happiness of their future lives, for gold? Will *you* make yourselves responsible for all the future miseries of your children, and your children's children, by recommending such a sordid compact? Forbear, I entreat you, for your own sake, for your children's sake, and for the sake of society, to recommend a marriage, which is not founded on pure, and strong, and mutual attachment.

Young people themselves, should be extremely careful on their own part to let no persuasions of others, no impulse of their own covetousness, no anxiety to be their own masters and mistresses, no ambition for secular splendour, induce them to enter into a connexion to which they are not drawn by the solicitations of a pure and virtuous love. What will a large house, splendid furniture, a gay equipage, and fashionable entertainments do for their possessor, in the absence of connubial love? " Is it for these baubles, these toys," exclaims the wretched heart as it awakens, alas! too late, in some sad scene of domestic woe, " is it for this I have bartered away myself, my happiness, my honour?"

" How ill the scenes that offer rest,
And heart that cannot rest agree."

O there is a sweetness, a charm, a power to please, in pure and mutual affection, though it be cherished in the humblest abode, and maintained amidst the plainest circumstances, and has to contend with many difficulties, compared with which, the elegance and brilliance of worldly grandeur, are but as the splendour of an eastern palace, to one of the bowers of the garden of Eden. Let the man nobly determine to earn his daily bread by the sweat of his brow, and find his daily task sweetened by the thought that it is for the woman he loves, rather than roll about in his chariot, and live a life of splendid indolence and misery, with the woman he does *not* love: and let the other sex, as nobly and heroically determine to trust to their own energies, but especially to a gracious Providence, rather than marry without affection for the sake of a settlement.

Then there is another error committed by some; having been disappointed in a connexion which they hoped to form, they become reckless for the future, and in a temper of mind bordering upon revenge, accept the first individual who may present himself, whether they love him or not. This is the last degree of folly, and is such an act of suicidal violence upon their own peace, as can neither be described nor reprobated in terms sufficiently strong. This is to act like the enraged scorpion and to turn their sting upon themselves; and in an act of spleen to sacrifice their happiness to folly. But in fact, on whom does this mad spite fall? Upon the individual who has done them no harm, but that of attempting to heal the breach that has been made in their happiness, and to whom in return they carry a heart which they have virtually given to another. How much more rational, how much more conducive to their own comfort, and how much more honourable is it in a case like this, to wait till time and piety have healed the wound, and left the heart at liberty for another attachment; and even to remain in perpetual celibacy, rather than marry without that which alone can constitute a virtuous marriage,—sincere affection.

Marriage should ever be contracted, WITH THE STRICTEST REGARD TO THE RULES OF PRUDENCE. Discretion is a virtue, at which none but fools laugh. In reference to no subject is it more frequently set aside and despised, than in that, which of all that can be mentioned, most needs its sober counsels. For love to be seen standing at the oracle of wisdom, is thought, by some romantic and silly young people, to be a thing altogether out of place. If *they* only were concerned, they might be left to their folly, to be punished by its fruits: but imprudent marriages, as we have already considered, spread far and wide their bad consequences, and also send these consequences down to posterity. The understanding is given to us to control the passions and the imagination; and they who in an affair of such consequence, as choosing a companion for life, set aside the testimony of the former, and listen only to the voice of the latter, have, in that instance at least, forfeited the character of a rational being, and sunk to the level of those creatures who are wholly governed by appetite, unchecked by reason. Prudence would prevent, if it were allowed to guide the conduct of mankind, a very large portion of human misery. In the business before us, it would allow none to marry till they had a prospect of support. It is perfectly obvious to me, that the present generation of young people, are not distinguished by a discretion of this kind : many are too much in haste to enter the conjugal state, and place themselves at the heads of families, before they have any rational hope of being able to support them. As soon almost as they arrive at the age of manhood, whether they are in business or not, before they have ascertained whether their business will succeed or not, they look round for a wife, and make a hasty, perhaps an injudicious, selection. A family comes on before they have adequate means of maintaining it ; their affairs become embarrassed ; bankruptcy ensues ; their prospects are clouded for ever ; they become burdens upon their friends ; and their misery, together with that of the partner of their folly, and of their hapless children, is sealed for the term of their existence upon earth. How many instances of this kind have we known, and which may be considered as sad, and true, and impressive comments on the imprudence of improvident marriages. Let young people exercise their reason and their foresight ; or if they will not, but are determined to rush into the expenses of housekeeping, before they have opened sources to meet them, let them hear, in spite of the syren song of their imagination, the voice of faithful warning, and prepare to eat the bitter herbs of useless regrets, for many a long and weary year after the nuptial feast has passed away.

Prudence forbids all *unequal* marriages. There should be an equality as near as may be in AGE; "for," says Mr Jay, " how unnatural, how indecent, is it to see an old man surrounded with infants and babes, when he can scarcely see or hear for the infirmities of age! How unnatural, how odious is it to see a young man fastened to a piece of antiquity, so as to perplex strangers to determine whether he is living with a wife or a mother." No one will give the woman in the one case, or the man in the other, the credit of marrying for love; and the world will be ill-natured enough, and one can hardly help joining in the censoriousness, to say that such matches are mere pecuniary speculations; for generally speaking, the old party in the union, is a rich one; and as generally they carry a scourge for the other in their purse. A fortune has often thus been a misfortune for both.

Equality of RANK is desirable, or as near to it as possible. Instances have occurred in which respectable men have married servants, and yet maintained their respectability, and enjoyed a full cup of domestic comfort: but these cases are rare and generally contain some circumstances of peculiarity. And it is much less perilous for a rich *man* to descend into the vale of poverty for a wife, than it is for a rich *woman* to go down for a husband. *He* can much more easily raise his companion to his own level, than *she can*. Society will much more readily accommodate themselves to his error, than to hers. Much of the happiness of the conjugal state, depends upon the relatives of the parties, and if the marriage has offended them, if it has degraded them, how much of bitterness is it in their power to throw into the cup of enjoyment. Many a wife has carried to her grave the sting inflicted upon her peace, by the insults of her husband's friends : and in all such cases, *he* must receive a part of the venom.

"It has been said that no class of men err so much in this article, as ministers. But surely this cannot be admitted. It cannot be supposed that those whose office it is to inculcate prudence, should themselves be proverbial for indiscretion. It cannot be supposed that those whose incomes are limited, and whose circumstances demand economy, would bring into the management of them, those who have been trained up in delicacy and extravagance; and are helpless and profuse. It cannot be supposed that men, whose office is respectable, and productive of social intercourse, would select vulgarity and ignorance, unfit to be either seen or heard, merely because it is pious. A minister is to inculcate order and regularity; and would he marry a female that would render his house a scene of confusion and tumult? A minister is to shew how the claims of life and religion harmonize, and to assign to the duties of each, their own place and season; and would he marry a rattle brain, who, instead of being a keeper at home, has been always rambling after some new preacher; who instead of quietly glorifying God in her own sphere of action, has been endeavouring to excite public attention; who has been zealous in matters of doubtful disputation, but has treated, as beneath her regard, matters of common and relative obligations? Need he be told, that a becoming behaviour in a lower and private station, is the surest pledge of, and the best preparation for, a proper behaviour in a higher and more private situation! A minister is to recommend neatness, and all the decencies of life, and would he marry a slattern? A minister is to shew, that the ornament of a meek and quiet spirit, is in the sight of God, of great price, and would he marry a scold? A minister is to stand in the same relation to all his people who demand his love and service, and would he marry a female who would fondly attach herself to a few cronies, listen to all *their* secrets, and divulge *her own*, and form cabals and schisms, which will render his residence unpleasant, or occasion his removal?"

To my brethren in the ministry I do recommend, and recommend with an earnestness which I have no language sufficiently emphatic to express, the greatest caution in this most delicate and important affair. In their case, the effects of an imprudent marriage, are felt in the church of the living God. If the wives of the deacons are to be "grave, not slanderers, sober, faithful in all things," what less can be required of the wives of the pastors? " A bishop must be blameless, one that ruleth well his own house, having his children in subjection with all gravity. For if a man know not how to rule his own house, how shall he take care of the church of God." But how can he exhibit in his domestic constitution, the beautiful order and harmony which should prevail in every christian family, and especially in every *minister's* house, without the intelligent and industrious co-operation of his wife: and how can this be expected of one who has no intelligence or industry? Not only much of the comfort, but of the *character* of a minister, DEPENDS UPON HIS WIFE; and what is of still greater consequence, much of his usefulness. How many have been driven away from scenes of successful labour, or rendered uncomfortable in the midst of them, by the mismanagement of wives, who have plunged their husbands into debt, and thus blasted their respectability: or by that pride, petulance, vulgarity, meanness, and busy interference, by which they have involved them in perpetual strife with their neighbours, tradesmen, or their congregation! Considering, therefore, how much mischief may be done by *their* indiscretion, ministers should raise imprudence in marriage to the rank of a great sin. And then their guilt in the commission of this sin is the greater, as they have less excuse for it than others; for they have only to exercise patience, and to restrain themselves from hasty and injudicious entanglements, and to avail themselves of the extended opportunity which their situation gives them, to obtain a companion that shall be to them, both as men and ministers, a helper of their joy. Some widowers in selecting a second wife have consulted their children's comfort more than their own taste; whether this be right or wrong in their case, we shall presently consider; but certainly a minister while he is allowed the usual privilege of following his own predilections, ought never to gratify his taste, at the expense of his official respectability, or at the risk of his usefulness, but in the choice of a wife, should be guided by a view to the comfort of his church, as well as by a reference to his own happiness.

Marriage should always be formed, WITH A DUE REGARD TO THE DICTATES OF RELIGION. A pious person should not marry any one who is not also pious. It is not desirable to be united to an individual even of a different denomination, and who, as a point of conscience, attends her own place of worship. It is not pleasant on a sabbath morning to separate, and go one to one place of worship, and the other to another. The most delightful walk that a holy couple can take, is to the house of God in company, and when, in reference to the high themes of redemption and the invisible realities of eternity, they take sweet counsel together. No one would willingly lose this. But oh to walk separately in a still more important and dreadful sense! To part at the point where the two roads to eternity branch off, the one to heaven, the other to hell; and for the believer " to travel on to glory, with the dreadful consciousness, that the other party is journeying to perdition!!" This is indeed dreadful, and is of itself sufficient to occasion no small diminution of conjugal felicity. If however, the comfort of the parties only were concerned, it would be a matter of less consequence: but it is a matter of *conscience*, and an affair in which we have no option. " She is at liberty to marry whom she will," says the apostle, speaking to the case of a widow, "but only in the Lord." Now though this was said in reference to a female, all the reasons of the law belong with equal force to the other sex. This appears to me to be not only advice but *law*, and is as binding upon the conscience as any other law that we find in the word of God; and the incidental manner in which this injunction occurs, is, as has been very properly remarked, to the intelligent reader of scripture, the strongest confirmation of the rule in all cases, where marriage is in prospect, and where there has been no engagement previous to conversion. As to the other passage, where the apostle commands us not to be unequally yoked together with unbelievers, it does not apply to marriage, except by inference, but to church fellowship, or rather to association and conduct in general, in reference to which, professing christians are not to symbolize with unbelievers. But if this be improper in regard to other matters, how much more so in that connexion which has so powerful an influence over our character, as well as our happiness. For a christian, then, to marry an individual who is not decidedly and evidently a pious person, is a direct opposition to the word of God.

And as scripture is against it, so also is reason; for " how can two walk together, except they be agreed." A difference of taste in *minor matters* is an impediment in the way of domestic comfort: but to be opposed to each other on the all important subject of religion, is a risk, even as it respects our comfort, which no prudent person should be induced, on any considerations, to incur. How can the higher ends of domestic constitution be answered, where one of the parents has not the spiritual qualifications necessary for accomplishing them? How can the work of religious education be conducted, and the children be trained in the nurture and admonition of the Lord? And as it respects individual and personal assistance in religious matters, do we not all want helps instead of hindrances? A christian should make every thing bend to religion, but allow religion to bend to nothing. This is the one thing needful, to which every thing should be subordinate; and surely, to place out of consideration, the affairs of his eternal salvation, in so important an affair as marriage, shows either that the religion of a person who acts thus, is but profession or likely soon to become so.

The neglect of this plain and reasonable rule is becoming, I am afraid, more and more prevalent. I do not wonder at all, that this subject should have excited the attention of the ministers of religion, and that the CONGREGATIONAL ASSOCIATION FOR WILTSHIRE should at their yearly meeting, in eighteen hundred and six, have come to the following resolution;—
" Deploring the little regard of late years paid by too many professors of religion to the christian rule of marriage; and deeming it desirable, that the attention of the public in general, and our own churches in particular, should be called to this subject; we do unani-

mously request the Rev. W. Jay to publish some strictures upon it."

In the excellent treatise which Mr. Jay published in compliance with this request, he makes the following just and important remarks. "How deplorable is it that this christian rule of marriage is so frequently trampled upon. The violation is, in the *degree* of it at least, peculiar to our own age. Our pious ancestors, especially among the non-conformists, would have been shocked at the practice, as appears from their invaluable writings. AND I AM PERSUADED THAT IT IS VERY MUCH OWING TO THE PREVALENCE OF THESE INDISCRIMINATE AND UNHALLOWED CONNEXIONS, THAT WE HAVE FALLEN SO FAR SHORT OF THOSE MEN OF GOD WHO ARE GONE BEFORE US, IN OUR SECLUSION FROM THE WORLD, IN THE SIMPLICITY OF OUR MANNERS, IN THE UNIFORMITY OF OUR PROFESSION, IN THE DISCHARGE OF FAMILY WORSHIP, AND IN THE TRAINING UP OF OUR HOUSEHOLDS IN THE NURTURE AND ADMONITION OF THE LORD."

No one should contemplate the prospect of such a connexion as marriage, without the greatest and most serious deliberation; nor without the most earnest prayer to God for direction. Prayer, however, to be acceptable to the Almighty, should be sincere, and should be presented with a real desire to know and do his will. Many, I believe, act towards the Deity, as they do towards their friends; they make up their minds, and then ask to be directed. They have some doubts, and very often strong ones, of the propriety of the step they are about to take, which are gradually dissipated by their supplications, till they have prayed themselves into a conviction that they are quite right in the decision, which they have, in fact, already made. To pray for direction in an affair which we know to be in opposition to God's word, and on which we have already resolved to act, is adding hypocrisy to rebellion. If there be reason to believe that the individual who solicits a christian to unite herself with him in marriage, is not truly pious, what need has she of praying to be directed? This seems like asking the Almighty to be permitted to do that which he has forbidden to be done.

In the case of WIDOWS and WIDOWERS, especially where there is a family, *peculiar prudence* is necessary. I have known instances in which such persons have sacrificed all their own tastes and predilections, and have made their selection with *exclusive* reference to their children. Such a sacrifice is indeed generous; but it may become a question whether it is discreet. It is placing their own comfort, and even character, in some degree of peril, neither of which can be lost without most serious mischief to those very children whose interests they have so heroically consulted. This, however, is an error much more rare and venial than that of the opposite extreme. How unseemly and inconsiderate is it for a sexagenarian, to bring home a young wife, and place her over daughters older than herself, and introduce into the family circle aunts and uncles, younger than some of the nephews and nieces. Rare is the case in which such inexpedient connections are formed, without the authors of them loosing much of their own reputation, and destroying much of the comfort of their families. Let not such men wonder, if their daughters by the first marriage, are driven from their home by the consequences of the second; and are led to form imprudent matches, to which they were led by the force of parental example, and urged by the consequences of parental folly.

In the selection of a second companion for life, where the first had been eminent for talents or virtues, much care should be taken that there be no great and and striking inferiority, for in such a case,

>——"Busy, meddling memory,
>In barbarous succession, musters up
>The past endearments of their softer hours;"

which form a contrast ever present, and ever painful. The man that never knew by experience the joy of a *happy* marriage, can never know the ills of an imprudent one, as aggravated by the power of comparison. Let him that *has* thus known them, beware how he expose himself to such helpless, hopeless misery.

Due care should also be exercised in reference to the children's interests. Has the woman about to be selected, that principle, that prudence, that self-control, that good temper, which, if she become herself a mother, will help her to conceal her partialities, for to suppress them is impossible, and would be unnatural, and to seem no less kind to her adopted offspring, than to her own? That man acts a most cruel, a most wicked, part towards the memory of his first wife, who does not provide for *her* children, a kind and judicious friend in his second. What is it but a dread of this that has made some women, when upon their dying bed, break through the rules of propriety, and recommend their successor in the arms, and heart, and house of their husbands? They trembled for their children, and seemed at that sad moment, to have become willing to be forgotten, provided their babes could find a second mother in her that was to fill their place. Let me then become the advocate of fatherless or motherless children, and entreat, for the sake, both of the living and the dead, a due regard for the comfort of these orphans.

Nor should less deliberation be exercised by the party who is about to take, or invited to take the care of another person's children. Have they love enough for the parent, to bear the burden of care for his sake? Have they kindness enough, temper enough, discretion enough, for such a situation, and for such an office? There is no difficulty where the children are lovely in person, and amiable in temper; but when they have no personal attractions, no charms of mind, no endearments of character, then is the time to realize the truth of Mr. Jay's expression, " a wife *may* be supplied, a mother *cannot*." The man or the woman that can act a parent's part towards a froward and unlovely child, must have more than *nature*, for this belongs only to a real parent, they *must* have principle and kindness, and *need* have grace. Let all who are invited to take the superintendence of a family, ask themselves, if they possess the requisites for the comfortable and satisfactory discharge of its duties. Let them enquire whether it is likely they can be happy in such a situation themselves; for if not, they had far better never enter it, as their unhappiness must inevitably fill the whole family circle with misery.

It cannot be sufficiently deplored, that all suitable preparation for the marriage state, is usually put aside for the busy activities of vanity, which in fact are but as dust in the balance of the conjugal destiny. Every thought, and anticipation, and anxiety, is too often absorbed in the selection of a house, and furniture; and in matters still more insignificant and frivolous. How common is it for a female to spend those hours day after day, and week after week, in communion with her milliner, debating and discussing the subject of the colour, and form, and material, in which she is to shine forth in nuptial splendour, which ought to be employed in meditating the eventful step, which is to fix for life her destiny, and that of her intended husband; as if the great object were to *appear* a gay and fashionable bride, rather than to *be* a good and happy wife. And most pitiable is it to see some mothers ministering to this folly, and flattering the vanity of their daughters, instead of preparing them by judicious and seasonable counsels, for discharging the duties of that new and important connexion, into which they are about to enter.

"Study," says an old author, "the duties of marriage before you enter into it. There are crosses to be borne, there are snares to be avoided, and manifold obligations to be discharged, as well as great felicity to be enjoyed. And should no *provision* be made? For want of this, result the frequent disappointments of that honourable estate. Hence that repentance which is at once *too soon* and *too late*. The husband knows not how to rule; and the wife knows not how to obey. Both are ignorant, both conceited, and both miserable."

IN ALL THY WAYS ACKNOWLEDGE HIM, AND HE SHALL DIRECT THY PATHS.

CHAPTER V.

THE DUTIES OF PARENTS.

"Ye fathers provoke not your children to wrath; but bring them up in the nurture and admonition of the Lord.
              EPHES. vi. 4.

"Train up a child in the way he should go, and when he is old he will not depart from it."
              PROVERBS, xxii. 6.

"And these words which I command thee this day, shall be in thine heart, and thou shalt teach them diligently unto thy children, and shalt talk of them when thou sittest in thine house, and when thou walkest by the way, and when thou liest down, and when thou risest up."
              DEUT. vi, 6. 7.

"And he shall turn the heart of the fathers to the children, and the heart of the children to the fathers, lest I come and smite the earth with a curse.
              MAL. iv. 6.

IT is an interesting and important era in the history of domestic life, when the husband and wife receive the new names of father and mother, and become united by the supplemental tie which is furnished by the little helpless stranger, so lately introduced into the family. Who that has felt them, can ever forget the emotions awakened by the first gaze upon the face of his child, by the first embrace of his babe? Little, however, do the bulk of mankind consider what a weight of obligation, what a degree of responsibility that child has brought into the world with him for his parents. In the joyousness with which the mother lavishes her fond embraces upon her boy, and in the paternal pride with which the father looks on this new object of their affection, how rarely does either of them revolve in deep seriousness, the future destiny of this new idol of their hearts; or consider how nearly that destiny is connected with their own conduct. Parental obligations are neither felt nor known by multitudes. How then can they be discharged? Rushing into the connexion of marriage under the mere impulse of passion, without forethought, without prudence, multitudes become parents, before they have one right view, or one right feeling, in reference to the duties of the parental relationship; to which they come with scarcely any other preparedness, than that mere animal fondness for their young, which they partake of in common with the irrational creation; but not with that same instinctive ability, "to train them up in the way they should go." Who can wonder at the disordered state of society at large, or be surprised at the aboundings of evils and miseries in our world, that looks at the manner in which domestic duties are neglected? When I consider what poor, ignorant, thoughtless, frivolous, wicked creatures are often seen at the head of households, I can only ascribe it to the interference of an all-wise and powerful Providence, that society is not far more chaotic than it is.

My business in this chapter is to endeavour to rectify, if possible, some of these evils, and to lay down a rule to guide the parent in discharging his truly important, and awfully responsible obligation; persuaded as I am, that many of the evils and miseries of society would vanish before a right performance of parental duties.

1. It is impossible for parents to discharge their duty, without a correct view of the nature and design of the domestic constitution.

This they should study, and arrive at the conclusion as speedily as possible, and keep it ever before the mind, that the great design of this compact is, *to form well the character of the children;* to train up the citizen for the world, and the christian for the church; to assist the child, as a mortal, to go with honour and comfort through this life, and as an immortal, to reach life everlasting. The domestic circle is intended to be the school of character, where, in the highest sense of the term, the most important business of education is to be conducted; where the moral sense is to be implanted and cultivated, and the conscience, and the temper, and the heart, are all to be trained.

2. Parents should be most deeply impressed and affected with a sense of the importauce of the station they occupy in the domestic constitution.

Their state of mind should be the very opposite of that light and frivolous indifference; that absence of all anxiety, which many of them manifest. There are some who seem to regard their children as pretty little living playthings, that must be well taken care of, and be taught, by somebody or other, whatever will set them off to the best advantage: but as to any idea of the formation of their character, especially of their moral and religious character, and any of that deep and painful, and almost overwhelming, solicitude, which arises from a clear perception and powerful impression of the probable connexion between the child's destiny and the parent's conduct, to all this they are utter strangers. Many horticulturalists have far more intense solicitude about the developing of their plants, far more wakeful and anxious care about the fragrance and colour of a flower, or the size and flavour of a fruit, than many parents have about the developement of mind, and the formation of character in a child. They have plants of immortality in their house, they have young trees which are to bear fruits to eternity, growing up around them, the training of which is committed to their care, and yet have very little solicitude, and scarcely any thoughtfulness, whether they yield in this world or the next, poisonous or wholesome produce. On parents it depends in a great measure what their children are to be,—miserable or happy in themselves; a comfort or a curse to their connexions; an ornament or a deformity to society; a fiend or a seraph in eternity. It is indeed an awful thing to be a parent, and is enough to awaken the anxious, trembling enquiry in every heart, "Lord, who is sufficient for these things?"

3. Parents should seek after the possession of all possible qualifications for their office.

What man in his senses would undertake the office of a pilot upon a dangerous coast, without a knowledge of navigation? Or that of a general of an army, without a knowledge of military tactics? Or that of a physician, without a knowledge of medicine and diseases? And who would go on another hour in the office of parent, without seeking to possess all suitable qualifications? And what are they?—

Genuine personal religion: for how can they bring up children in the nurture and admonition of the Lord, if they do not know the Lord for themselves? In order to teach religion with any probable effect, we must know it ourselves. That parent will have little ability, and less inclination, to inculcate piety upon his children, who has none himself. A graceless parent is a most awful character! Oh! to see the father and mother of a rising family, with a crowd of young immortals growing up around them, and teaching irreligion to their offspring, and leading them to perdition, by the power of their own example. A sheep leading her twin lambs into the cover of a hungry tiger, would be a shocking sight; but to see parents by their own irreligion, or want of religion, conducting their family to the bottomless pit, is most horrible!! No one, then, can rightly discharge the duties of a parent, in the higher reference of the family compact, without that personal religion which consists in repentance towards God, faith in our Lord Jesus Christ, and a life of habitual holiness. In the absence of this, the highest end of the domestic constitution *must* be neglected, the sublimest part of education must be abandoned.

Parents should seek the *entire government of their temper :* a habit of self-control ; a meekness not to be disturbed by the greatest provocation ; a patience not to be wearied by long continued opposition. I say to any father or mother, are you irritable, petulant ? If so, begin this moment the work of subjugating your temper. You are in iminent peril of ruining your family. A passionate mother or father, is like a fury, with a sceptre in one hand, and a firebrand in the other ; and when the king is a fury, the subjects are likely to be furies too ; for nothing is more contagious than bad temper. O how many parents have had to bewail with weeping eyes and almost broken hearts, the effects of their own irritability as apparent in the headstrong, passionate dispositions of their children. It is against this evil that the admonition of the apostle is directed, " *forbearing threatening.*" Passion blinds the judgment, leads to undue severity, fosters partialities, in short, is the source of a thousand evils in the domestic government. An irritable person can never manage discipline with propriety, but is ever prone to correct, when correction should never be administered, in a rage. Parents, I beseech you to control your temper, and acquire a calm, imperturbable disposition, for this only can fit you to rule your household in wisdom, justice, and love.

A habit of discrimination is a very important qualification in parents: a penetrating insight into character; an acuteness in judging of motives. Such a talent is of immense consequence in the domestic community; and connected with this, a quickness of discerning disposition, together with an inventive and ingenious faculty of adapting treatment to the varieties of character and propensity which are continually exhibiting themselves.

A kindness of manner, an affectionate, persuasive address is of great importance. It is desirable for parents to render their company pleasant to their children, to engage their confidence, to exert over them the influence of love, which certainly cannot be done by a cold, or churlish, or distant behaviour.

Prudence and good sense are qualities of such inestimable worth, and depend so much upon education, that all who have the care of children, should perpetually exhibit them for imitation. A rash, thoughtless father, or a wild, romantic mother, do incalculable mischief in a family.

Firmness is essentially requisite in parents; that disposition, which, though at the remotest distance from all that is rigid, stern, and cruel, can master its own feelings, and amidst the strongest appeals to the tenderer emotions of the mind, can inflexibly maintain its purpose; and in the way of denying improper requests, or administering correction, can inflict pain on the object of its affection, whenever duty requires such an exercise of beneficial severity. For want of this disposition, of this fine and noble quality, how many have ruined their children for ever by indulgence.

Varied information and extensive knowledge are very desirable. Parents should be able to direct the studies, to answer the enquiries, to correct the mistakes, to regulate the pursuits, and in short, to superintend the general instruction of their families.

Unvarying and inflexible consistency should be exhibited by all whom providence has placed at the head of a household. They should be not only excellent, but *consistently* excellent. An unbroken uniformity should reign over their whole character. Nothing contradictory, inexplicable, irreconcileable, should ever be seen.

Let all who are likely to become parents, look at this picture and learn how they are to prepare for the performance of their duty ; and let those who already sustain this relationship, correct their errors and supply their defects by this rule.

4. Parents should settle, with themselves, what is their chief desire and highest object of pursuit, in reference to their children.

Without fixing on some end, we shall never in any course of action, proceed with much steadiness, comfort, or success : and where many ends are, and may be with propriety contemplated and sought, the *chief* one must be definitely selected, and continually kept in view, or we shall ever be in danger of misapplying our energies. Let parents, then, consider the ends which they should propose to themselves, in reference to their children, and decide among all those that are lawful, which is supreme, and which are subordinate.

There are *many* lawful ones, but only one of these can be supreme. And what is that? RELIGION. What christian can for a moment hesitate here? What genuine believer can for a moment question whether his children's eternal salvation ought to be the supreme solicitude of his heart? If we look to the great bulk of mankind it is perfectly evident that religion hardly enters into their view; they are very willing that their children should go to church or to meeting, according as they themselves are church people or dissenters, but as to any anxiety about the religious character, the formation of pious habits, they are as destitute of every thing of this kind, as if religion were a mere fable, or were nothing more than a mere sabbath day form. Their chief object is, either elegant and fashionable accomplishments, or learning and science, or perhaps prudence and good sense; and provided their sons and daughters excel in these, they never make any enquiry or feel any anxiety whether they fear God; and would be not only surprised, but would either laugh you to scorn, or scowl upon you with indignation, for proposing such fanatical or methodistical questions in reference to *their* children. Yes, this is the way of the greater part of parents, even in this *religious* country. To train them up to shine and make a figure in society, is all they seek. Amazing folly! Dreadful and murderous cruelty! Degrading and grovelling ambition! To lose sight of the soul, and neglect salvation, and forget immortality! To train them in every kind of knowledge but the knowledge of religion, to instruct them in an acquaintance with every kind of subject, but to leave them in ignorance of God their Creator, their Preserver and Benefactor ! To fit them to act their part well on earth, and to leave them unprepared for heaven ! To qualify them to go with respectability and advantage through the scenes of time, and then to leave them unmeet for the glorious and enduring scenes of eternity ! O strange fondness of irreligious parents ! O miserable destiny of their hapless offspring !

In direct opposition to this, the chief end of every christian parent must be the spiritual interests, the religious character, the eternal salvation of his children. Believing that they are sinful and immortal creatures, yet capable of being redeemed through the mediation of Christ, his highest ambition, his most earnest prayer, his most vigorous pursuit should be engaged for their eternal welfare. His eye, his heart, and his hope, should be fixed on the same objects for them, as they are for himself, and that is, upon eternal life. This should be the nature and exercise of his anxiety; " I am desirous, if it please God, that my children should be blessed with the enjoyment of reason, of health, of such a moderate portion of worldly wealth, and worldly respectability as is compatible with their station in life, and with a view to this I will give them all the advantages of a suitable education; but above and beyond this, I far more intensely desire, and far more earnestly pray, and far more anxiously seek, that they may have the fear of God in their hearts, may be made partakers of true religion, and be everlastingly saved. And provided God grant me the latter, by bestowing upon them his grace, I shall feel that my chief object is accomplished, and be quite reconciled to any circumstances which may otherwise befal them ; for rather would I see them in the humble vale of poverty, if at the same time they were true christians, than on the very pinnacle of worldly grandeur, but destitute of true piety." Such should be the views and feelings and desires of all true christian parents; religion should be at the very centre of all their schemes and pursuits for their offspring. This should be the guiding principle, the directing object, the great land-mark by which all their course should be steered.

Having made these preliminary remarks, I go on to enumerate and illustrate the various branches of parental duty.

FIRST. There are some which relate more directly TO THE PRESENT LIFE, AND THE FORMATION OF THE CHARACTER GENERALLY.

1. *Maintenance* is of course a claim which every child justly prefers upon his parents, till he is of sufficient age to be able to provide for himself.

2. *Scholastic instruction* is another duty we owe our children. The dark ages are happily passed away, and a flood of light is now poured, and is still pouring over all classes of the people. Instruction is become general, and even they who are too poor to buy knowledge for their children, are not ashamed to beg it in

our sunday and charity schools. No man should suffer his family to be in this respect, behind the age in which they live. To grudge the money spent in this way is a cruel and detestable niggardliness. A good education is a portion, the only one which some are able to give to their children, and which in many cases, has led to every other kind of wealth. In this, however, we are to be guided by our rank in life and circumstances; and for a labouring man, or a small tradesman, to impoverish himself in order to procure the same kind and degrees of accomplishments for *his* children, as a rich man and a nobleman would for their's, is an ambition sanctioned neither by reason nor revelation. Where it can be accomplished, parents should prefer domestic instruction, to sending their children away from home: no school can possess the advantages which are to be enjoyed under the eye of a judicious father or mother. But how few *are* judicious; how few are equal to the task of a general superintendence of the business of instruction; and how few can command the advantages of it at home. Let all such *be careful in the selection of a school,* for it is a matter of infinite consequence. Let them be guided in their choice, not by a mere regard to accomplishments, not by a view to the best drawing, dancing, music, or Latin master. This is an age of gaudy, exterior decoration. But let them first regard *religion,* then, *the real cultivation of the mind* and the *formation of good habits.* Wherever real piety is inculcated, a thirst for knowledge excited, and habits of appplication, reflection, sobriety of judgment, and good sense are formed, that is the school to be selected by a wise and christian parent. No word is more abused than that of EDUCATION, which in the mind of many, signifies nothing more than the communication of knowledge. But this is only a part, and a small part, of education, which, in fact, means the formation of character. A youth may have his head stuffed full of Latin, Greek, mathematics, and natural philosophy; a girl may draw, and dance, and play, and speak French exquisitely, and yet be miserably educated after all. Integrity, good sense, generosity, and a capacity for reflection, are worth all the acquirements which even an university can bestow. Not, however, that these are incompatible with each other; by no means: and the perfection of education is the union of both.

3. *A due regard to the health of children* should be maintained.

Physical education is of no small importance. Knowledge gained at the expence of health is purchased at a dreadful rate. And there are other ways of injuring the health of children, besides a too close application of learning, for this indeed but rarely occurs. Fond and foolish mothers should be warned against pampering their appetites with sweets, corrupting their blood with grossness, or impairing the tone of their stomachs with fermented liquors. Infanticide is practised even in this christian land, by many who never dream that they are child murderers: they do not kill their babes by strangling or poisoning them; no, but by pampering or stuffing them to death. And where they go not to this extreme, they breed up a circle of gluttons, or drunkards. Nothing can be more disgusting than to see children invited to eat all the delicacies of the dinner, and to drink after it the health of the company, with what their young palates ought to be strangers to. And lamentably injudicious it is to make the gratification of the appetite a reward for good conduct, and to have them ushered into the parlour, before they retire to rest, to receive the luscious sweet, which is the bribe for their going quietly to bed. The mischief goes beyond the corruption of their health, for it brings them up to be governed by appetite, rather than by reason; which is, in fact, the secret cause of all the intemperance and profligacy of the world. Settle your plans on this subject, and suffer neither a favourite servant, nor a kind aunt, nor a doating grandpapa, to come between you and the welfare of your children.

4. *Bring up your children with low notions of the importance of riches and worldly show, and of the power which these things have either to give respectability to the character, or to procure happiness.*

Do not let them hear you magnify the value of wealth by your words, nor see you do it by your actions. Avoid an obsequious attention to the rich and great; point not to *them* as the individuals most to be admired and envied. Discover no undue solicitude about grandeur of abode, or furniture. From the time that they are capable of receiving an idea, or an impression, teach them it is CHARACTER that constitutes true respectability : that a good man is reputable in any circumstances, a bad man in none. Remind them of the danger of riches, and that they are satan's baits to tempt men to love the world, and lose their souls. Not that you should produce a cynical disposition towards either riches or the rich ; much less repress industry, and foster indolence ; no : but encourage them to consider and seek wealth, rather as a means of usefulness, than a source of personal gratification.

5. *Inculcate industrious habits.*

Caution them against sauntering and slothfulness. From the dawn of reason endeavour to convince them not merely by argument, but by a reference to their own experience, that employment is pleasure, and idleness misery. Impress them with the value of time ; that it is the stuff of which life is made, and that we lose as much of life as we do of time. And connected with this, enforce habits of order and punctuality. The parent that neglects to do this, is guilty of enormous unkindness towards his children ; who, if they grow up without these, incommode themselves, and are a source of prodigious inconvenience to their friends.

6. *Economy* is no less necessary. Industry and economy are virtues of civilized life. Savages never possess them, but spend their time in idleness, and squander what comes in their way in wastefulness. It is reason overcoming the vis inertiæ which is natural to man, that produces industry and economy ; and when we consider how important they are to the well

being, not only of individuals, but of society, our efforts should be employed to foster them in the minds of our children. But, in inculcating economy, we must be careful not to drive the mind into covetousness; hence it is of consequence, that with all our endeavours to cherish frugality, we should be no less assiduous to encourage generosity; and to impress them with the idea, that the end of saving, is not to hoard, but to distribute to the wants of others.

7. *Provide for your children suitable employment.* Happily the pride and indolence of feudal times are gone by, and it is our felicity to live in a country where trade and industry are accounted honourable, and where the aristocracy softens down into the democracy by almost insensible degrees; where a poor, proud gentleman, that scorns the vulgarity of trade, begins to be thought a very despicable character; and the diligent, honest, and successful tradesman, regarded as an honourable member of the community. " The good, sound common sense of mankind will never annex character to a useless life. He who merely hangs as a burden on the shoulders of his fellow men, who adds nothing to the common stock of comfort, and merely spends his time in devouring it, will be invariably, as well as justly accounted a public nuisance." Let parents therefore, take care to bring up their children to some suitable business; in the selection of which, due regard should be had to their own circumstances; for it is great folly and unkindness also to select for a child a business, so much above his

father's station and property, as to leave no rational hope that he can ever enter upon it with a prospect of success. In the advance of society we see innumerable instances of foolish pride of this kind: and indeed it is a pretty general thing for parents to be ambitious to obtain for their children a higher grade in society than their own. Many who have really acquired wealth in a reputable, though perhaps not the most genteel trade, (for trades have their aristocratic distinctions,) seem anxious that their sons should be a step higher than themselves, and instead of sending them to business, look out for a profession, and there is a wondrous rage for professions in the present day: or if they are retail tradesmen, must make their sons wholesale ones; or if they are manufacturers must start them as merchants; and if they are merchants, must elevate them into gentlemen. What abject folly is it for a man to turn away the attention of his children from any good and honourable business, which *he* has followed with success, merely because it is not genteel. I believe that great harm has been done by an injudicious system of education, which has become *too exclusively classical*. Literature, when kept within due bounds, and properly united with mercantile branches, does not in itself unfit a youth for business; but it is considered as the acquirement of those who are intended to be professional men or gentlemen: and when almost exclusively pursued to a late period in boyhood, it turns off the attention from business, and partially unfits for it. A very undue importance has been attached in our schools to polite literature, to the neglect of science and commercial knowledge. Let every christian tradesman, who has a business worth following, keep as many of his sons as he can at home with him, and educate them himself for trade in his own warehouse. Due attention must, of course, always be paid in the selection of a business, to the physical strength, to the mental capacity, and to the prevailing taste of a child.

8. *Generosity* should be most assiduously inculcated.

All children, and consequently all mankind, are more or less selfish by nature. This should be early watched and checked by a judicious parent, and an opposite disposition inculcated. Even infants may be made to feel the pleasure of sharing their possessions with others. Let them be taught that enjoyment arises not from individual gratification, but from a communion in pleasure. As children advance in years and reason, they should hear much of the happiness arising from gratifying others; of the luxury of benevolence, and of the meanness of greediness. We should descant on the beauty of generous actions, and of beneficent examples. Anecdotes of remarkable generosity should be read to them, and especially should we dwell upon the wondrous love of God, and the remarkable compassion of Jesus Christ. We should send them on errands of mercy to the poor and needy, that being spectators both of their misery, and of their tears of gratitude for relief, they might acquire a disposition to do good. We should especially encourage them to make sacrifices, and practice self-denial, to do good. To give them *extra* money, in order that they may relieve the poor, or support religious institutions, is doing them very little good ; for this is only being generous at other people's expence ; but they should be induced to save their own pocket money, and distribute their regular allowance, and thus forego the gratification of their own palate, for the purpose of relieving the wants of others. But they should never be *compelled* to give, never have their money stopped for this purpose; never be fined for misconduct, and have their fines appropriated to charity; for all this is calculated to disgust them with benevolence.

Great care should be taken at the same time, not to induce a habit of indiscriminate distribution, which would render them the dupes of hypocrisy, the subjects of imposition, and the victims of extortion. We should teach them the difference between real benevolence and that easy good nature, which allows itself to be wheedled out of every thing; between the generosity of a correct judgment, and that of a weak and credulous mind; between principle and mere feeling.

9. *Prudence* is of vast consequence in the affairs of life. This is, next to piety, the most valuable quality of character. Nothing can be a substitute for it; and it does more for the comfort of its possessor, more for the happiness of society than any other attribute of mind that can be mentioned. Half the miseries of some persons' lives, who are good people too, arise from a rash, thoughtless, indiscreet mind. They never think

before they speak or act: they have no power, or exercise none, of forethought, deliberation, or calculation. Such persons are firebrands, without intending it; and commit immense mischief, without, perhaps, a particle of malice. How important, then, that children should be early taught the nature and value of discretion. Many parents most egregiously err on this subject: some are anxious only to communicate knowledge; forgetting that ideas are worth nothing, but as they are discreetly employed to produce happiness. Knowledge is only the materials of comfort; it is wisdom that must put them together into form and consistency. Others almost despise prudence; it is not a classical, a scientific, a poetic quality. It cramps genius, extinguishes taste, prevents the lofty, though somewhat erratic flights of an ardent mind; it is cold and calculating; it has nothing sublime or romantic about it; it never soars into the clouds, or plunges into the depths, but holds on its dull course on the low level of ordinary concerns. And therefore, just on this very account, it is the very thing to be coveted. Foolish, foolish creatures! And so you would have your children geniuses, that disdain the restraints of wisdom, and resemble mere fire works, that burn and blaze out only to please others by their brilliancy and splendour, without doing good to any one! O be not so cruel to yourselves, to your children, to society. Teach them to cultivate a deliberative, a reflecting, a calculating judgment; to weigh their words, and measure their actions; enforce upon them a habit of looking onward to the tendency and results of conduct; the calm and regular government of the soul, which leads its possessor to observe true measures, and a suitable decorum in words, and thoughts, and actions. Give them all the learning you can procure for them; I quarrel not with this: but in your own estimation, and in all your conduct towards them, exalt wisdom far above learning, genius, taste, accomplishments; and in this sense of the word, teach them *that the price of* WISDOM *is above rubies.*

Now I am anxious to impress upon the mind of all parents, that the inculcation of these dispositions, forms in fact, the very essence of education. This term, as I have already remarked, and I repeat the sentiment again and again, not by accident or oversight, but with the design of more deeply impressing it, has been very generally misapplied, because, in fact, misunderstood. Education in modern parlance, means nothing more than *instruction*, or the communication of knowledge to the mind; and a *good* education means, the opportunity of acquiring all kinds of learning, science, and what are called accomplishments. But properly speaking, education in the true and higher import of the term, means the implanting of right dispositions, the cultivation of the heart, the guidance of the temper, the formation of the character. Or allowing, as we must, that education applies to the whole soul and character, and includes general instruction in knowledge, I should say that its most important part is that which relates to the communication of active principles, and the formation of moral habits.

It is TRAINING UP A CHILD IN THE WAY HE SHOULD GO. Not merely the training up a child in the way he should think, or speculate, or translate, or dance, or draw, or argue, but the way in which he should *go*. Every thing may be taught which can sharpen the faculties, or store the mind with ideas, or cultivate the taste ; but we must not stop here, but consider that the highest end of education, is the formation, first of the religious character, and then of the useful, amiable, intelligent, and generous member of the social community.

If this be true, and who will venture to deny it, then is it perfectly manifest, that the great work of education cannot be, and ought not to be transferred from parents to others. They may purchase that tuition which their own circumstances may disqualify them from imparting, but the education of the character belongs to *them*, and cannot be transferred. Here I cannot resist the temptation of introducing a long extract from Mr. Anderson's incomparable work.

" Placed by the all-wise providence of heaven in such a peculiar situation, it will be well for you to keep especially in view, what may be denominated, THE EDUCATION OF CIRCUMSTANCES. Let purchased tuition be carried up to the very highest perfection, and let neither money nor wisdom be spared in reaching this height; of such vital importance in the training of children, is that department to which I now refer, that it can, and if neglected will, undermine and undo the whole, as well as render many efforts in educating the disposition, altogether abortive. Suffer me to explain my meaning.—

" In the laudable anxiety of their hearts, two parents with a family of infants playing around their feet, are heard to say, ' Oh ! what will, what can best educate these dear children ?' I reply, ' Look to *yourselves* and your *circumstances*.' Maxims and documents are good in themselves, and especially good for the regulation of *your* conduct and your behaviour towards them : but with regard to your children, you have yet often to remark, that many maxims are good precisely till they are tried, or applied, and no longer. In the hands of many parents, they will teach the children to talk, and very often little more. I do not mean to assert, that sentiments inculcated have no influence ; far from it ; they have much ; though not the most ; but still, after all, it is the sentiments you let drop occasionally, it is the conversation they overhear, when playing in the corner of the room, which has more effect than many things which are addressed to them directly in the tone of exhortation. Besides, as to maxims, ever remember, that between those which you bring forward for their use, and those by which you direct *your own* conduct, children have almost an intuitive discernment : and it is by the latter they will be mainly governed, both during childhood and their future existence.

" The question, however, returns, ' What *will* educate these children ? And now I answer, ' Your example will educate them—your conversation with your friends—the business they see you transact—the likings and dislikings you express—*these* will educate them; the society you live in *will* educate them—your domestics *will* educate them: and whatever be your rank or situation in life, your house, your table, and your daily behaviour, these, *these* will educate them. To withdraw them from the unceasing and potent influence of these things is impossible, except you were to withdraw yourself from them also. Some parents talk of *beginning* the education of their children; the moment they were capable of forming an idea, their education was already begun—the education of circumstances—insensible education, which, like insensible perspiration, is of more constant and powerful effect, and of far more consequence to the habit, than that which is direct and apparent. This education goes on at every instant of time; it goes on like time—you can neither stop it nor turn its course. Whatever these, then, have a *tendency* to make your children, that, in a great degree, *you* at least should be persuaded they will be.

" The language, however, occasionally heard from some fathers, may here not unseasonably be glanced at. They are diffuse in praise of maternal influence; and pleased at the idea of its power and extent, they will exclaim, ' O yes, there can be no doubt of it, that every thing depends upon the mother.' This, however, will be found to spring from a selfish principle, and from anxiety to be relieved from mighty obligations, which, after all, cannot be transferred from the father's shoulders, to those even of a mother : to say nothing of the unkindness involved in laying upon her a burden, which nature never intended, and never does. Her influence, as an instrument, indeed, a husband cannot too highly prize; but let no father imagine, that he can neutralize the influence of his own presence, and his own example at home. He cannot if he would, nor can he escape from obligation. The patience and constancy of a mother, are no doubt, first mainly tried, but *then* those of the father. The dispositions in each parent are fitted by nature for this order in the trial of patience; but from the destined and appropriate share allotted to each, neither of the two parties, when in health, can relieve the other.

" Addressing myself, therefore, to both parents, I would say, ' Contract to its just and proper dimensions, the amount of all that purchased education can do for you, and expect no more from it than it is truly able to perform. It can give instruction. There will always be an essential difference between a human being cultivated and uncultivated. In the department of purchased tuition, you will portion out to the best advantage, many of those precious hours of youth which never will return; and such employment will lend you powerful aid in forming those personal habits, which lie within the province of parental education; but rest assured, and lay it down to yourselves as a cardinal principle, that the business of education, properly so called, is not transferable. You may engage a master or masters, as numerous as you please, to instruct your children in many things, useful and praiseworthy in their own place, but you must by the order of nature, *educate* them yourselves. You not only ought to do it, but you will perceive that if I am correct in what I have stated, and may still advance, you *must do it whether you intend it or not.*' 'The parent,' says Cecil,' ' is not to stand reasoning and calculating. God has said, that his character *shall* have influence; and so this appointment of Providence becomes often the punishment of a wicked or a careless man.' As education, in the sense I have explained, is a thing necessary for all,—for the poor and for the rich,—for the illiterate as well as the learned, Providence has not made it dependant on systems, uncertain, operose, and difficult of application. Every parent, therefore, save when separated altogether from his family, may be seen daily in the act of educating his children: for from father and mother, and the *circumstances* in which they move, the children are daily advancing in the knowledge of what is good or evil. The occupations of the poor man at his labour, and of the man of business in his counting house, cannot interrupt this education. In both instances the mother is plying at her uninterrupted avocations, and her example is powerfully operating every hour; while at certain intervals daily, as well as every morning and evening, all things come under the potent sway of the father or the master, whether that influence be good or bad. Here, then, is one school from which there are no truatns, and in which there are no holidays.

" True, indeed, you send your children to another

school, and this is the very best in the whole neighbourhood, and the character of the master there, is not only unexceptionable, but praiseworthy. When your children come home too, you put a book of your own selection into their hands or even many such books, and they read them with pleasure and personal advantage. Still, after all this, never for one day forget, that the first book they read, nay, that which they continue to read, and by far the most influential, is that of their parents' example and daily deportment. If this should be disregarded by you, or even forgotten, then be not at all surprised when you find another day, to your sorrow and vexation, and the interruption of your business, if not the loss of all your domestic peace and harmony, that your children only ' know the right path, but still follow the wrong."

SECONDLY.—But I now go on to illustrate and enforce those duties which parents owe to their children IN REFERENCE TO THEIR RELIGIOUS CHARACTER, AND THEIR ETERNAL WELFARE.

Not that religion is to be taught separately from all other branches of education, as an abstract thing of itself, for *it is not* an abstract thing of itself, but an integral part of the character, the substratum of all the qualities that have been already stated. " Bring them up in the fear and nurture and admonition of the Lord:" this is all the apostle enjoined on the subject of education, and it is the substance of all we are to teach : whatever is opposed to this must not be taught, and all that is taught or enjoined must be inculcated with a direct or indirect reference to this. In the selection of a school even for obtaining the elements of general knowledge in the branches of tuition that he permits his children to be taught, a christian parent must have his eye upon religion, and this must be the polar star by which he steers.

Still, however, for the sake of making the matter more clear and obvious, as the subject of solemn obligation, I place religious education by itself: and it includes—

1. INSTRUCTION.

As soon as reason dawns, religious instruction should commence. The subject matter of instruction includes every thing which forms the fundamental points of revealed truth: the character of God, the spirituality of his law, the fall of man, the evil of sin, the person and work of Christ, the need of repentance, the justification of the soul by faith, the nature and necessity of regeneration, the operating power of love to Christ as the spring of obedience, the solemnities of judgment, the immortality of the soul, the punishment of the wicked, and the happiness of the righteous: all these should be familiarly taught according as the capacity is able to receive them. Our instruction should not be confined to mere generalities, but should proceed from the beginning, on evangelical principles. The basis of our teaching should be the bible itself. Not that I would totally discard all catechisms. I do not see why definitions and explanations—and what else are the answers in catechisms?—may not be as useful in religion, as in any other subject. Catechisms are injurious only when they push out the bible, not when they lead to it. Still I admit, that the bible should be the text book. Every child should learn a portion of scripture daily, and have it explained to him. A great prominency in all our instruction should be given to the *law* of God, as binding the conscience, and the consequent exceeding sinfulness of every human being; together with the wonderful grace of the Lord Jesus Christ as the sinner's only Saviour. Much use should be made of the historical parts of scripture, as illustrating by its facts the character of God, the evil of sin, the consequences of disobedience. Abstract principles alone will not do. Children like facts, and must be taught through the medium of their imagination. Instruction must be conveyed *in a pleasing form.* In order to this, there must be no wearying them by long lectures; no disgusting them by long tasks. I reprobate the practice, as a most injurious one, of setting a long lesson of catechism or scripture to a reluctant child, and then punishing him for not learning it. If we wish to disgust their minds with the ways of godliness, this is the way to do it. Many an injudicious parent, in the very act of teaching piety towards God, calls into existence and activity the very tempers which it is the design of religion to suppress. An angry and scolding father, with a catechism in one hand, and a rod in the other, railing at a stubborn child for not learning his lesson, is not a scene very calculated to invest religion with an air of loveliness and a power of attraction for young minds: the only association which in such a circumstance a child can be expected to form with learning to be pious, is that of a dark room or a cane; pain of body and insufferable disgust of mind. I would say to many a parent " do give over the business of teaching religion, till you can command your temper, and attract the child to the subject as that which is agreeable. *Never set religious tasks to your children as penalties for bad conduct.* To be made to learn catechism or scripture, in solitary confinement, and upon an empty stomach, and thus to connect imprisonment and fasting with the penance, is a sure way to finish the aversion which the rod has commenced. Instead of compelling a child to learn religion because he is naughty, which is reversing the order of things, he ought not to be permitted to touch so holy a thing in so evil a temper.

Instruction, to be valuable, must always be delivered with *great seriousness.* The light and trifling way in which it is sometimes delivered destroys all its effect, and reduces it to the level of a mere science. It ought not to be exclusively confined to the Sabbath, but be the business of every day; yet it should be especially attended to on the day of rest, when the family should be interrogated, as to what they understand and remember of the sermons they have heard in the house of God. Children cannot too early be made to comprehend the purpose for which they go up to public worship, and that *they* have a personal interest in all the sacred services of our religious assemblies.

No parent who has a numerous family, and who resides in a large town, where much time must necessarily be occupied in going to, and returning from his place of worship, should attend the house of God more than twice on the Sabbath: the other part of the day should be occupied in the midst of his family. This is far too generally neglected in this day of overmuch preaching.

Instruction should be *adapted to the capacity of the children,* and keep pace in depth and variety, with the strengthening of their faculties. Provide for them suitable books; and as they advance in age, enter with them more into the depths of theological truth; unfold to them the beauty, the grandeur, and sublimity of revelation; instruct them in the evidences of the bible; the proofs of its fundamental doctrines. I am not very fond of boys and girls writing religious themes, or conducting any researches of a religious nature, as a mere exercise of ingenuity, except their minds are already well disposed towards religion as a matter of personal experience.

2. PERSUASION, ADMONITION, AND WARNING, are a very important part of religious education.

The apostles, " knowing the terrors of the Lord," *persuaded* men; they besought them to be reconciled to God; and warned them of the consequence of unbelief. Parents must do the same with their children, and not satisfy themselves with merely communicating ideas. They should, in the most earnest, anxious, affectionate manner, represent to them their spiritual condition, warn them of the consequences of neglecting the great salvation, and intreat them to believe in the Lord Jesus Christ, and fear God. They should address them collectively and individually, on the subject of their souls' concerns; they should manifest such a deep solicitude for their spiritual welfare, as would constrain their children to feel that the most anxious desire of their parents' hearts, in reference to them, is their salvation. This should not however be done merely when their children have offended them; nor should they, on every slight occasion of misconduct, have a ready recourse to the terrors of the Lord. Parental authority must not be supported exclusively by the thunders of heaven, or the torments of hell. These subjects should never be referred to, but in seasons of solemn and affectionate admonition. It would also be prudent not to be so frequent in the business of admonition, warning and persuasion, as to excite nausea and disgust. Many good, but injudicious people, completely overdo the matter, and defeat their own purpose; they worry the children on the subject of religion, and thus increase the aversion that is already felt. Nothing in the way of bitter reproach, or of railing accusation, for the want of piety, should ever be uttered; nor should anger ever be manifested. In the case of elder branches of the family, a word or two occasionally spoken, and always in great mildness and tenderness, is all that is desirable. Incessant remonstrance, is in such instances, likely to be heard with indifference, if not with dislike. Such young people should be left pretty much to their own judgment and conscience, and to the force of parental example.

3. *Discipline* is unspeakably important. We have considered the father as the *prophet* of his family, we are now to view him as their *king;* and his laws are as important as his instructions. By discipline, then, I mean the maintenance of parental authority, and the exercise of it, in the way of restraining and punishing offences. Parents, you are invested by God himself with an almost *absolute* authority; you are constituted by him the supreme magistrate of your household, and cannot have a right idea of your situation, without considering yourself as appointed to *rule*. You *must* be the sovereign of the house, allowing no interference from without, no resistance from within. You have no option in the matter, and are not permitted to abdicate the throne, or to cast away your sceptre. It was mentioned as a high commendation of Abraham that he would *command* his children after him. But although you are to be absolute monarch, uniting in yourself the legislative and executive department, you are to be no tyrant. Your government must be firm, but mild: the love of the parent must not relax the reins of the governor, nor the authority of the governor diminish ought from the love of the parent. You must have a sceptre, and always hold it, but it should not be an iron one. You must never suffer the yoke to be thrown off from your children, but then it should be a yoke which they shall have

no *inclination* to throw off, because it is easy, and the burden light. Of you in *your* measure, it should be said, as it is of God,

>"Sweet majesty and awful love
>"Sit smiling on his brow."

Your authority must be presented to your children as soon as reason is awake. The first thing a child should be made to understand, is that he is to do, not what he *likes,* but what he is commanded; that he is not to govern, but to be governed. The sceptre should be seen by him before the rod; and an early, judicious and steady exhibition of the former would render the latter almost unnecessary. He must be made to submit, and that while young, and then submission will become a habit; if the reins be felt by him *early,* he will thus learn to obey them. All commands should be *reasonable :* there should be no wanton, capricious use of authority, we must not thwart and cross the wills of our children merely to teach submission. They should perceive clearly that love is at the bottom of all we do, and that reason guides all our conduct. We should calculate before hand, whether there is a necessity for the injunction we are about to deliver, and a probability of our being able to ensure compliance; for a wise parent will not enjoin any thing, if he can help it, that has not these circumstances connected with it. Commands should be sacred things, not issued in sport for the child to play with. Nothing but what is wise should be enjoined, and every injunction that is issued should be obeyed. In many cases, it is beyond our power to ensure obedience; and then nothing remains but punishment.

Correction is an essential part of discipline; for rewards and punishments are as necessary in the government of a family, as in that of a state. What saith the wisest of men? " Foolishness is bound up in the heart of a child, but the rod of correction will drive it far from him. Withhold not correction from the child: for if thou beatest him with a rod, he shall not die. Thou shalt beat him with a rod, and shall deliver his soul from hell. The rod and the reproof give wisdom: but a child left to himself bringeth his mother to shame." Do not many mothers know this by bitter experience? Even in lesser matters, have they not a thousand times blushed at the rudeness, ill manners, and impertinence of children " left to themselves:" and in *greater* matters, have they not lived to vent the heaviest reproaches upon their most abject folly, in spoiling their children, by leaving them to their own obstinate tempers, self-will, and rebellious conduct, without ever correcting them: " Correct thy son, and he shall give thee rest; yea, he shall give thee the delight of thy soul." Inimitably beautiful precept; and as true as it is beautiful. " He that spareth the rod, hateth his son." How many are there who thus hate their children? A very strong expression, I admit; and yet these very persons would be thought the fondest of parents. Would you suffer your children's bodies to perish, rather than put them in pain in eradicating a disease, which if suffered to remain would be fatal? Would not *this* be hating them? And what do you call that conduct, which, rather than put them to pain by correcting their faults, suffers all kinds of moral diseases to increase, and fester, and corrupt the soul? Fond mother, you that will never correct a child, hear the charge, and let it thrill through your heart, exciting emotions of horror —you are a hater of your child; your foolish love is infanticide; your cruel embraces are hugging your child to death. In not correcting him, you are committing sin of the heaviest kind, and your own wickedness, in not correcting *him*, will at last correct yourself.

I would not, however, be thought to enjoin a cruel or even a stern and rigid severity. I do not think this compatible with the admonition given by the Apostle, not to irritate, nor "provoke our children to wrath, lest they be discouraged." We must not *govern by punishment:* the sceptre must not be converted into a whip. The first object of every parent should be to render punishment unnecessary. It is better to prevent crimes than punish them. This *can* be done, certainly, to a very considerable extent, but it requires a very early, very judicious, and very watchful system of training. Many have very little of what may be called, the faculty of government: and late coercion and punishment, come in to supply the place of early guidance. The only time is suffered to go by without being improved, in which it is possible in most cases, so to train the disposition, as to do in future without much punishment: for if discipline, wise, steady, firm discipline, do not commence as soon as the passions begin to develope, it is too late then to be accomplished without some degree of severity.

Mr. Anderson strikingly illustrates this part of the subject, by a very familiar allusion : I recollect hearing of two coaches which used to drive into Newmarket from London, by a certain hour, at a time of strong competition. The horses of the coach which generally came in first, had scarcely a wet hair. In the other, though last, the horses were jaded and heated to excess, and had the appearance of having made great efforts. The reader, perhaps, understands the cause of the difference. The first man did it all, of course, by the *reins;* the second, unsteady in himself, or unskilful in the reins, had induced bad habits, and then employed the *whip;* but he could never cope with the other. So it will ever hold in all government. If obedience to the reins is found to be most pleasant in itself, and even the road to enjoyment, then obedience will grow into a habit, and become, in fact, the choice of the party."

This, then, is the first thing to be attended to: acquire skill in the management of the reins ; govern by guiding, not by forcing. But still, there are many, very many cases, in which the reins alone will not prove to be enough ; the whip is wanted, and where it *is* wanted, it ought to be supplied. Not that I mean to enforce a system of *corporeal* punishment; no: this may be necessary occasionally, *as an experiment* in difficult cases; but as a *system* it is bad and unavailing, and is usually the resource of passionate, ignorant, or indolent parents and masters. We should, from the dawn of reason, endeavour to make our children feel that our favour is their richest reward for good conduct, our displeasure the severest rebuke for misbehaviour. Happy the parent, who has attained to such skill in government, as to guide with a look, to reward with a smile, and to punish with a frown.

Occasions, I admit, sometimes do occur, and not unfrequently, in which the interposition of a severer chastisement becomes necessary; and these are the emergencies which require the full stretch of parental wisdom. Take the following rules for your guidance: —Never chastise in a state of wrath. Some parents can never punish except, when it ought never to be done, when they are angry. This is passion, not principle; and will always appear to the child as if it were intended, more to appease and gratify the parent's bad temper, that to promote *his* welfare. No parent, in such a state of mind, can be in a condition nicely to adjust the kind and degree of punishment to the offence; it is like administering medicine scalding hot, which rather burns than cures. God waited till the cool of the evening before he came down to arraign, try, and punish our first parents after their fall.

Patiently examine the offence before you punish it.

In every case, let there be the solemnity of judicial investigation; for justice always should proceed with a slow and measured step. Accurately discriminate between sins of presumption, and sins of ignorance or inadvertence. Accidents should be reproved, but not punished, unless they involve wilful disobedience. Most wisely and equitably apportion the sentence to the degree of offence and the disposition of the offender. Ingenuous confession, and sincere penitence, should in most cases arrest the process of judgment, and the child be made to punish himself by remorse. Satisfy not yourselves till you have produced repentance, for till you have done this, scarcely any thing is done. Hatred of the sin, on the part of the offender, is a much more effectual preservative from its repetition, than fear of punishment. Do not keep instruments of punishment, such as the rod or the cane, constantly in sight, for this is to govern by fear, rather than by love. Be very cautious not to threaten what you either did not intend, or are not able to inflict; yea, forbear threatening as much as possible. A parent's denouncement should not be hastily uttered for children to laugh at. In the case of older children, the greatest caution is necessary, in expressing a parent's displeasure; reasonable expostulation, mild rebuke, tender reproof, appeals to their understanding, and feelings, and conscience, are all that can be allowed in this instance. If beating ever do good, it is only in infancy, before the understanding can be made sufficiently to argue upon the heinousness of the offence; afterwards it can only provoke and harden. Through the whole course of discipline and government, let parents ever remember, that their children are *rational* creatures, and are to be dealt with as such, by having the grounds of obligation laid open to them, the criminality of disobedience explained, and the evils of insubordination laid before them. To a parent storming or fretting over the inefficacy of punishment, I would say, "Have you treated that child as a brute, or a rational creature? Have you taken pains with him from infancy, to make him understand his obligations, and to comprehend the criminality of disobedience; or have you governed him by threatening and beating?" I again say, that where *necessary* punishment is withheld, it is a hating of the child, but the great object should be to render punishment *unnecessary*. Put the *reins of guidance* upon the disposition while your children are infants, and acquire great skill in these: and if you manage the reins well, you will have less need of the whip.

It is of vast consequence that parents should be very careful not to foster, by injudicious treatment, those very propensities, which when more fully developed, they will find it necessary to repress by discipline. Do not encourage lying and ill nature, by smiling at a false, or malignant expression, because it is cleverly said: nor nourish pride by excessive flattery or commendation: nor vanity, by loading them with finery, and both admiring them, and teaching them to admire themselves: nor revenge, by directing them to vent their impotent anger upon the persons or things that have injured them: nor cruelty, by permitting them to torture insects or animals: nor insolence and oppression, by allowing them to be rude to servants: nor envy, by stimulating too powerfully the principle of emulation. Infinite mischief is done by thus thoughtlessly encouraging the growth of many of the germs of vice.

Discipline to be effectual, should be *steady* and *unvarying*, not *fitful* and *capricious:* it must be a system, which, like the atmosphere, shall press always and every where upon its subjects. Occasional fits of severity, however violent, but which are followed by long intermissions of relaxing indulgence, can do no good, and may do much harm. Each extreme is mischievous, and each prepares for the mischief of the other. *Both parents should join* to support domestic authority; for a more truly distressing and injurious spectacle can scarcely be seen in the family circle, than a fond and foolish mother counteracting the effects of paternal chastisement, by stealing to the little prisoner in his captivity, to comfort him in his distress, to wipe away his tears, and to hush his sorrows, by some gratification of his palate. In this way children have been sometimes hardened in their crimes, set against their father, and led to ultimate and irretrievable ruin.

Wonder not that I have placed discipline under the head of *religious* education; for is it not the object of domestic government to bend, as far as means can do it, the will of a child into submission to the authority of a wise and holy parent? And what is sin against God, but the resistance of a weaker will against that which is supreme and divine? Now surely it may be conceived to be in the order of God's appointed means of bringing the child into subjection to himself, to bring him first into subjection to his parents. Can any one be in a state of mind more hardened against religion, more opposed to all its just and salutary restraints, than he who rejects the mild yoke of parental government, and sets at defiance the authority of a father? Obedience to parents is one of the laws of heaven, and the first of all its laws which the mind of an infant can be made to understand; and if parents enforce it as they should do, with a direct reference to the appointment of God, they are certainly taking a preliminary step, so far as means can be employed, for the formation of the religious character.

4. EXAMPLE is necessary to give power and influence to all other means.

One of the tritest of all proverbs, is the power of example; but its force is greatest upon the youthful mind: "During the minority of reason, imitation is the regent of the soul, and they who are least swayed by argument, are most governed by example." We all learn of this preceptor, before we can reason, and before we can speak. If then we would have our children live in the fear of God, we must ourselves be seen by them steadily walking in the way of his commandments. In alluring them to religion, we must be enabled to say, " Follow me." Our religion should not only be upon the whole sincere, but it should be *visible:* our light should shine before our family, that they seeing our good works, may glorify God. But for our religion to produce any effect, it must be *eminent:* there must be no doubt, no uncertainty about the matter; it must not be a thing of a questionable nature. It should be *consistent.* I remember once conversing with a man of great eminence for station, talents, and piety, who said to me, " I owe every thing, under God, to the eminent and consistent piety of my father. When I was a young man, though I was not vicious, I was worldly; and in order the more effectually to get rid of all interference with my pursuits from religion, I wished to think it all mere profession and hypocrisy. For this purpose I narrowly watched the conduct of my father; for such was the height on which he stood as a professor of religion, that I very naturally concluded, if I could convict him of such inconsistency as amounted to a proof of hypocrisy, and a little thing would at that time have sufficed for such a purpose, I should have gained my end, and have concluded that all piety was but a name and a delusion. But so thoroughly consistent was he, that I could find nothing in the smallest degree at variance with his character as a professor of religion. This kept its hold upon me. I said to myself there must be a reality here, and I must try to understand and feel it; for I have seen such meekness in a temper naturally irritable, such comfort amidst the greatest agonies, and all this supported by such uniform devotion, that I must try to catch his spirit." This beautiful instance of the influence of parental example is, perhaps, not altogether unique: though in all its circumstances, perhaps rarely equalled.

Children have their eyes always upon their parents, and are quick to discern any violations of consistency. If notwithstanding our profession of religion, they see us as worldly minded, as grasping and anxious after riches, as solicitous to be surrounded by splendid furniture, luxurious gratifications, and fashionable habits, as the people of the world;—if they see the righteous rarely at our table, except when they are great people, or popular characters, but on the contrary observe there the gay, the fashionable, the ungodly; —if they witness us artful, implacable, or malicious; —if they know us to be cruel or neglectful to our wives, unkind and oppressive to our servants, cold and tyrannical to them;—if they witness us inconstant in our attendance upon private, family, or public worship—what can they conclude but that our religion is mere profession? In such a case, of how little service is our attempt to impress upon their minds those claims which we ourselves practically deny? It were far better for some parents to say nothing to their children about religion, for till they alter their own conduct, their admonitions can produce no other effect than to excite insufferable disgust. It is enough to make every parent tremble, to think what a parent should be.

And there should be consistency also, between our professions and our conduct, in reference to our families. We avow it to be our supreme and ultimate desire, that *they* should be truly pious; and we tell them so. Do we in all things act agreeably to this principle? Do we select schools and situations, books and companions, pursuits and occupations, in reference to this desire? Do we in our general conversation *with* them, and *before* them, support this declaration? Do not our children sometimes reason thus?—" My parents tell me that their chief anxiety is for my salvation, and the formation of my religious character; but how does this comport with their selecting for me a school where religion is the last thing attended to? With their instructing me in some things, which, as religious people, I hear them condemn? How is it that all the anxiety of their conduct, whatever their words may say, appears to be to make me a fine lady, that can dance well, and exhibit an elegant form, and display polished manners? I am told that *religion* is the first thing, but I am educated for the *world*." Ah, if we act thus, we are not training up our children in the way they should go. Without example, every thing else that we do, is most lamentably deficient: as has been often said, it is only pointing them the way to heaven, but leading them in the way to hell.

5. Diligent, constant, and careful inspection, is a most important parental duty.

There should be in every family, a system of domestic episcopacy. Parents should be watchful in all things. This is the way to preserve the good seed of instruction which is sown, and to prevent the enemy from sowing tares, which he is ever wakeful to do when the parent is asleep. This is a very difficult, but a very necessary duty. We must never allow any engagements whatever to take off, long together, our eye from our children. As soon as their character begins to unfold, we should most carefully watch its developement, that we may know what regimen to place it under. We should study their propensities, capacities, and tendencies. We should watch them in play, in their intercourse with each other, with servants, with their companions, and when they are not dreaming that our attention is directed towards them; for character is decided by incidents, which a superficial mind would deem too minute to be noticed. We should see how they behave after punishment and reward: in short, their whole character should be studied and inspected by us, with the most minute and anxious care; just as the different plants in a nursery are investigated by a gardener, that he may know the peculiar nature which each possesses, and the appropriate treatment which each requires.

We should also inspect our family, so as to know what good or evil is going on among them: whether the good seed is growing, and what tares are springing up. Like the farmer going out to examine his fields, or the gardener his trees, to ascertain what prospect there is of a crop, and what weeds are to be eradicated, what vermin to be destroyed, what gaps to be stopped to keep out enemies, what excrescences to be removed, what assistance to be afforded;—so must the parent be and act among his children. One is growing up with a propensity to pride, *he* must be taught with great care, the beauty and excellence of humility; a second is vain of personal decorations and acquirements, *she* must have such folly exposed, and be saved from its injurious influence upon her character; a third is artful, equivocating and deceitful, *he* must have the enormity of lying unfolded to him, and be encouraged to practice more frankness, ingenuousness, and regard to truth; one is remarkably curious, and needs to have this inquisitiveness checked; another dull, and needs to have it stimulated; one is sceptical, and is in danger of infidelity; another credulous and is in peril of imposition. Now there must be a constant scrutiny carried on by the parent, to ascertain these peculiarities, and to manage them accordingly.

Inspection must extend to *every thing*. To the *servants* that are admitted into the house; for how much injury might be done to the youthful mind by an unprincipled and artful servant. The *companions* of our children should be most narrowly watched; one bad associate may ruin them for ever. The very first workings of the social impulse, even in a boy or girl of five or six years of age, should be noticed, for even thus early may evil impressions be produced by companionship. At the risk of offending the nearest relative, or most endeared friend he has upon earth, a christian parent ought not to suffer his children to associate with those who are likely to do them harm. On this account, domestic education is decidedly to be preferred, where it can be obtained, to schools. A system of extensive and dreadful mutual corruption is oftentimes going on among young people before it is perceived.

Parents should most carefully inspect the *reading* of their children, and keep out of their way all corrupting books and indecent pictures. And how deeply is it to be deplored, that our *newspapers* are oftentimes so polluted with filthy details of disgusting occurrences and trials, as to be channels through which moral contamination flows into many a family, otherwise well guarded. It becomes a serious question, whether it is the duty of a christian, who has sons and daughters growing up, to allow a newspaper to come into his house. Newsrooms on this account, are very valuable.

The *recreations* of children should be watched, and no games be allowed that are immodest, nor such as are likely to foster a spirit of gambling.

For want of this diligent, careful, and universal inspection, the best instructions, the most earnest warnings, the most fervent prayers, and the most consistent example, have been in some cases, unavailing : and the children left to themselves, and the corrupting influence of others, have grown up their parents misery, and their own disgrace.

6. PRAYER must crown all.

This duty commences with the birth of a child, nay, before that event; for in the very prospect of its birth, there should be earnest prayer offered to God by the parent, for divine grace to discharge all those obligations, which the expected babe will bring upon the conscience of the father and mother. And from that time forward, till the death of either parent or child, earnest, secret, believing prayer, should never cease to be daily presented for our offspring. Our prayers should principally respect the *spiritual* welfare of our children. Daily we should wrestle with God for their eternal salvation. How little can *we* do at most for their welfare, and how ineffectual without God's blessing, is all we do, or can do. That parent has neglected a very important branch of his duty, who has suffered one single day to pass by without bearing his children upon his heart before God in private prayer. Who can subdue their tempers or change their hearts, but God? And though in a way of sovereignty, he confers his grace upon some who neither seek it themselves, nor have it sought for them by their friends, yet we are not authorised to expect it without prayer.

It is necessary, also, not only to pray *for* our children but *with* them. We should take them apart, each by himself, to commend them to God, and thus make them the witnesses of our deep solicitude, and our intense agony for their eternal welfare. If they have been disobedient and wicked, it may be well, when they are brought to a right mind, and when we ourselves have forgiven them, to conduct them to the throne of divine grace, to beg for them the *divine* forgiveness: but this never must be done as a punishment, for this is the way to make them dread a parent's prayers, as a visitation of his displeasure.

But besides this, there must be FAMILY PRAYER.

The necessity and propriety of this, arise out of the constitution of the family; and were it not enjoined in the word of God, either by precept or example, would still be binding upon the conscience of every parent, by the relation in which he stands to his family, and the extent of their dependance upon God. Do we not want family mercies, and who can give them but God? So obviously obligatory is this duty, and so naturally does its performance arise out of all our conjoint feelings as parents and as christians, that those who neglect it, cannot even pretend to feel the right influence of godliness.

No duty, however, has been more abused than this. By some it is only *occasionally* performed; it is taken up, perhaps, in times of domestic distress or solicitude: by others, it is attended to on a sabbath evening; and by many, very many others it is, though regularly observed, nothing but a lifeless form, and thus felt not only to be insipid, but a mere burden. The following directions may be of service to guide the heads of families in this most interesting branch of domestic duty.

1. It should he offered up morning and evening, thus beginning and closing every day.

2. It should be observed with the greatest regularity, and an uninterrupted constancy. What a dis-

grace to a parent is it for a child or a servant to say, "Are we to have prayer this evening?" And yet, are there not some families in which the practice is so irregular, as to leave the matter doubtful, till the bell rings?

3. All the members of the family should be present, except very young children, who cannot be made to sit still, and whose inquietude and restlessness are a disturbance to all the rest, and utterly destroy the solemnity of the service.

4. It should be attended to so early in the morning as not to subject the service to the intrusion and interruption of visitors, and secular business; and so early in the evening, as not to be rendered the mere form of a drowsy circle, who ought at that time to be in bed. It is an offence to the Almighty to conduct a family into his awful presence, merely to sleep there.

5. There should be a fixed hour, and the hour should be most sacredly kept, and not to be interfered with, except at the dictate of necessity. In order to this, the heads of families should not sup from home, nor yield to the modern practice of late visiting. The fashionable hours of ten or eleven o'clock at night, are driving out *evening* prayer, and the eagerness of commercial pursuits putting a stop, in many families, to the *morning* sacrifice.

6. A portion of holy scripture should be read from the Old Testament one part of the day, and from the New Testament, the other. A book should be read through in regular course, and not a chapter picked

out, or stumbled upon by accident. The scriptures should be audibly read, and in a reverential manner, and with a devotional spirit, for very great evils result from reading the scriptures in a careless, slovenly, and irreverent manner. It would be well for the parent to require the children and servants to bring their bibles with them, that the eye may help the ear, in fixing the attention of the mind. The domestic prophet should also accompany what he reads with short explanatory and hortatory remarks of his own, or the expository comments of others.

7. Where there are persons in the family that can sing, family praise should be a part of the service. The morning or evening hymn of a pious family is one of the most touching sounds in our world.

> " Lord! how delightful 'tis to see
> " A *pious household* worship Thee:
> " At once they sing,—at once they pray;
> " They hear of heav'n, and learn the way."

8. Then follows the prayer, which should be not so long as to weary, nor so short as to seem like a mere form: it should be fervent; for a dull, cold, heartless repetition of almost the same things, in almost the same words, is sure to destroy all the interest of this delightful service, and render it a mere form, which wearies and burdens, if it do not also disgust. How difficult is it to keep up the life and vigour of this engagement! And why? Because we do not keep up the life and vigour of our own personal religion. It is worth while to remark, that the habit of reverential

H

reading the scriptures tends to feed the flame of devotion, and to kindle the fire of the sacrifice of prayer. The prayer of the head of a family should be in a very peculiar degree FAMILY prayer. It should respect the children, the servants, the circumstances of the household. All should feel that the service belongs to them, and not merely to the individual who prays, or to the church and the world. But fervour, and life, and earnestness, as opposed to what is dull and formal, are of immense consequence. A few petitions breathed forth with a fervour that kindles the fire of devotion in all around, are far better than half an hour's talking about religion to God.

Oh! with what dignity, and grace, and sanctity, and authority, does a holy and fervent father rise from his knees, and take his seat in the midst of his family, while yet the rays of divine glory play upon his countenance. "Children," says Dr. Dwight, "naturally regard a parent with reverence; but they cannot fail to reverence him more or less, on account of his personal character. Wherever they have been accustomed to behold their parent daily sustaining the office of minister or servant of God, they necessarily associate with every idea they form of his person and character, this solemn and important apprehension. Every image of this venerable relation presented to their minds, will include in it that of a divinely appointed guardian of their spiritual concerns; a guide to their duty given them from above; a venerated and beloved intercessor for their salvation." And the same writer in speaking of family worship, says, "In the devotion of this little assembly, parents pray for their children, and children for their parents; the husband for the wife, and the wife for the husband; while brothers and sisters send up their requests to the throne of Infinite Mercy, to call down blessings on each other. Who that wears the name of man can be indifferent here? Must not the venerable character of the parents, the peculiar tenderness of the conjugal union, the affectionate intimacy of the filial and fraternal relations; must not the nearness of relations long existing, the interchange of kindness long continued, and the oneness of interests long cemented,—all warm the heart, heighten the importance of every petition, and increase the fervour of every devotional effort."

It may be now proper to enquire, how it comes to pass that such a system as this is so often unsuccessful? For it may, with very great propriety, because with truth, be affirmed, that the families of professors are not always, as it might be expected they would be, the nurseries of the church. It is not enough to resolve the matter into the sovereignty of divine grace, till we have first enquired whether any thing can be found in the conduct of parents, which can be said with truth, to account for the painful fact of irreligious children being found in religious families.

Have parents really adopted and pursued a judicious system of religious education? Can it be said, that means, such as I have directed, or any thing at all like them, have been regularly pursued? Has there been a deep, a constant solicitude for the eternal welfare of their children?

In the introduction of my volume, entitled, "A Christian Father's Present to his Children," I have stated the obstacles which often prevent the success of a religious education, and have enumerated the following:—

1. Religious education is oftentimes very ignorantly, negligently, and capriciously maintained, where it is not altogether omitted. It is not a *first* object; it is attended to with no earnestness, no anxiety, no system, no regularity. It does not run through every thing, and is opposed by many things at variance with it. The parent's eye and heart are more intently fixed upon the worldly prosperity and respectability of the children, than on their religious character.

2. The relaxation of domestic discipline is a powerful impediment in the way of success. There is, in some households, no family government, no order, no subordination. The children are kept under no restraint, but are allowed to do what they like; their faults are unnoticed and unpunished, and their tempers allowed to grow wild and headstrong; till, in fact, the whole family become utterly lawless, rebellious against parental authority, and unamiable to all around them. How many have had to curse the over-indulgence of fond and foolish parents. How many, as they have ruminated amidst the desolations of poverty, or the walls of a prison, have exclaimed, " O, my cruelly fond parents, had you exercised that authority with

which God entrusted you, over your children, and had you checked my childish corruptions, and punished my boyish disobedience; had you subjected me to the salutary restraint of wholesome laws, I had not brought you with a broken heart to your grave, nor myself with a ruined character to the jail."

Over indulgence is awfully common, and continually making shocking ravages in human character. It is a system of great cruelty to the children, to the parents themselves, and to society. This practice proceeds from various causes; in some instances, from a perverted and systematic sentimentalism; in others, from absolute indolence, and a regard to present ease, which leads the silly mother to adopt any means of coaxing, and yielding, and bribing, to keep the young rebels quiet for the time; in others, from a mistake as to the time when restraint should begin, or a spirit of procrastination, which leads parents to say, " I shall take them in hand by and bye: there is no time lost; when their reason is a little more matured, I shall lay upon them more restraint:" and in some it is "mere animal affection," without the guidance of a particle of judgment; a mere instinct, like that which in the irrational tribes leads to a blind and busy care. It is not uncommon for parents to treat the first acts of puerile rebellion, rather as freaks to be smiled at, than as faults to be reformed. " O," says the mother, " it is only play, he will know better soon. He does not mean any harm. I cannot chide him." No; and if the father, wiser than herself, does, she cries, and perhaps, in the hearing of the child, reproves her husband for cruelty. From whatever cause it proceeds, it is in the highest degree injurious to the character of the children; let those who are guilty of it read the fearful comment on this sin, which is furnished for their warning in the history of Eli and his family.

3. Undue severity is, perhaps, more injurious than over-indulgence; and it is, perhaps, a conviction of this, and an observance of the mischievous consequences of extreme rigour, that has driven many into the opposite extreme. I have seen the dreadful effects of parental tyranny and the reign of household terror, in the broken spirits, the reckless desperation, the hardened contumacy, or the deep and sullen melancholy of those who have been the subjects of these hard measures. It is a truly revolting sight to see a *father* employing the iron rod of the oppressor to beat and bruise, and crush the minds of his own offspring into the most abject submission. He may succeed, but let him not wonder, if at the same time that he has suppressed rebellion, he has extinguished affection. I have known parents, who, too late have seen their error, and who would give the world, did they possess it, if it were possible to do away the ill effects which their severity had produced in the character of their children; but the mischief was irreparable. No subsequent kindness could expand the heart, which they had closed for ever against them, or win that confidence which they had repulsed from them. A close, sullen, melancholy disposition had been nurtured: a

susceptibility to the emotions of wretchedness had been planted in the bosom, which no future tenderness on the part of the parent could remove. He saw it, and repented it, but could not alter it. "Ye fathers, provoke not then your children to anger, lest they should be *discouraged.*" This language is really very striking, and well deserves the serious attention of every parent.

4. The inconsistent conduct of parents who are professors of religion, is a great hindrance to the success of religious education. Many persons have no need to wonder that *their* children are *not* pious; it would have been a wonder with every body else if they were, for they have seen nothing at home but what was calculated to disgust them with religion. They would have been far more likely to have thought well of the ways of godliness, if their parents had said nothing about them.

5. The bad conduct of an elder branch of a family often counteracts all the efforts made for the benefit of the rest. Let parents see the importance of *beginning* upon a good system. Children are creatures of imitation, and the models they copy after, are their elder brother or sister. A mother should educate the character of her *first* child, with the recollection, that he will be a pattern, which the rest will, in all probability, more or less conform to. I do not think this has been sufficiently considered.

6. Partiality has a very corrupting and fatal influence. The history of the patriarch Jacob, first the

victim, and afterwards the subject, of this sin, will remain for ever a warning to all parents, against the dangers of domestic favouritism. The balances of government must be held, in every family, by evenhanded justice, or misery is sure to ensue. Envy and jealousy are the natural consequences of partiality. Father and mother are sometimes embroiled, the children are set against each other, and all conspire against the favourite.

Behold these obstacles, and avoid them.

And now, can *motives* be necessary to admonish christian parents to the diligent performance of their duty? If so, take the following:—

1. Are you zealous for the cause of religion in the world,—for the prosperity of Zion,—for the interest of the Redeemer,—for the glory of God? Be diligent and anxious to train up your children in the nurture and admonition of the Lord. Would you have them the enemies, or the friends of God and his cause? Dare you pretend to be the disciples of Christ, if this is a matter of indifference to you? If you are neglectful in this matter, you may expect to see your offspring united with the children of this world, if not with infidels, scoffers, or the profane. But if you are anxious and conscientious to train them up for God, that daughter over whom you watch with such parental care and tenderness, may be joined with the female worthies, who by their chaste conversation, and the ornament of a meek and quiet spirit, and their zeal for the cause of Christ, have done so much to diffuse

religion in the world. That son whom you now train with such holy solicitude, for future usefulness, as a disciple of the Saviour, may become eminent in the church, as a consistent and intelligent member, or an able and faithful minister. "Many a congregation," says Baxter, " that is happily fed with the bread of life, may thank God for the endeavours of some poor man or woman, that trained up a child in the ways of God, to become their holy and faithful teacher." The church of God looks to the families of the righteous, and expects and asks from thence, those supplies which are to recruit its numbers, and to repair the ravages of death.

2. I urge this duty by a due regard to the temporal and eternal welfare of your children. You love your children, and would deem it a most cruel and insulting insinuation to have your affection for a moment questioned. But do what you will for them; devote as you may the energies of body and mind; the sleep of your nights and the activities of your days to your children's comfort: wear out your strength in ceaseless labour and solicitude, and yet at the same time neglect the religious education of your children, you are guilty of a species of most horrid cruelty towards them, the dreadful consequences of which may begin in this world in profligacy and vice, and extend to the other in all the bitter pains of eternal death. Unrestrained by sentiments of piety, uncontrolled by a conscience which has never been enlightened, what is to prevent them from being plunged into infamy by their unbri-

dled passions? Have not many young men, at the hulks, in the land of exile, or at the gallows; and many unhappy females when closing in misery a course of infamy, cursed their parents for not giving them a religious education? But even though they live and die in worldly honour and respectability, what will this do for them amidst the sorrows of life, the agonies of death, the solemnities of judgment, and the torments of perdition. Hear them as they stand shuddering and affrighted on the brink of that gulph into which they are about to plunge. "Of what avail are the riches and honours, and pleasures of the world, which my parents were so anxious to obtain for me? Why did they not tell me that the salvation of my soul was of more importance to me as an immortal creature, than the possession of the universe? Cruel, cruel parents! Fool that I was to be blinded and rendered careless by you: but my self-reproaches are now unavailing, I deservedly perish; but my blood be upon the head of those that neglected me." Ah, cruel parents indeed, who neglect the religious education of their children; more cruel in some respects than Herod; he slew the bodies of children, these murder souls; he murdered the children of others, these murder their own; he employed the agency of his servants, these do the work of slaughter themselves.

3. Do you regard your own comfort? Do you love yourselves? Are you anxious to avoid painful and incessant solicitude, bitter reflection, domestic disquietude, dreadful foreboding? Then bring up your chil-

dren with the most unvarying regard to their religious character. Should God crown your efforts with success, what a harvest of joys will you reap even in this world. When you see your children enter the paths of wisdom, "thank God!" you will exclaim, "my highest ambition has at length reached its object. My children are decided christians. I am now no longer distressingly anxious for their future prospects in this life. In one way or other, God will provide for them. And as to eternity they are safe." Who can describe the pure, elevated felicity with which such parents mark the course of their children, in going from strength to strength in their progress to Zion. What a season of delight is that, when they publicly assume the profession of a christian, and connect themselves with the church! What joy is felt on beholding them at their side at the table of the Lord, and holding communion with them in the joys of faith and the anticipations of eternity. And what satisfaction is experienced in seeing them enrolling their names as the friends of God and man, and giving their support to those institutions which are formed to promote the highest interests of the human race. As they grow in experience, in usefulness, in respectability in the church, the parents' joy and gratitude are continually increasing, and they feel the honour of having sent such members into the fellowship of the faithful. Should God, in the mysteries of his providence, remove them by an early death, you will be cheered amidst the agonies of separation, by their dying consolation; their piety will wipe away your tears, and be a balm to the wounds of your mind; and when they have departed, you will solace yourselves with the healing thought, that they are gone to that world of glory in which you will soon be reunited with them. Or should the order of nature be observed, and you precede them to the tomb, will not *their* presence and attentions in your dying chamber, be more soothing by the consideration, that they are so many saints, as well as children, ministering to your comfort? Will not their piety give a sanctity and a sweetness to all the offices of their affection? " I die," will be your expression, as like departing Jacob, you address yourselves to them, " but God will be with *you*, and we shall meet again where there will be no more death."

But should you unhappily neglect their religious education, and they, through your inattention, should grow up without any due sense of the claims of God, is there not a danger of their becoming immoral, as well as irreligious? And how could you bear to witness, or to hear of their profligacy and vice, if at the same time you were conscious that it was in a measure through your neglect? Perhaps they may be unkind and disobedient to you; for God may justly render that child a scourge to his parent, whose parent did not train him up in the ways of religion. O what scenes of domestic misery, what heart-rending spectacles of confusion and wretchedness, have profligate children occasioned in the families to which they belong! How many have thus had their hearts suddenly broken, or their gray hairs brought down by the slow process of withering sorrow to the grave; and the sting of all this, in some cases, has been the consciousness of parental neglect. No sin more heavily punishes itself, than this, nor mingles for its subject a more bitter cup. But then, the *eternal* consequences, oh! the eternal consequences of this neglect. See the heart-stricken parent, wringing his hands over the dying youth who is departing without repentance. No, not a syllable escapes his lips that sounds like penitence: the father weeps, and prays, and entreats, but the son hearkens not, and dies, and makes no sign. Now in what a burst of agony does he give vent to his feelings over the corpse, from which the spirit has departed, but departed not to the mansions of the blest. —"Oh, my son, Absalom, my son, my son Absalom, would God I had died for thee; O Absalom, my son, my son."

Or, in the event of your own death, what thorns will it plant in your pillow, with what deeper shades will it invest the descent to the dark valley, to reflect that you had forgotten the religious character of your children, and the eternal salvation of their immortal souls. *Then,* amidst these fearful scenes, to awake to a sense of your duty, when it it is too late, except by one parting admonition to perform it. *Then* to see those around your bed, with whom you had been entrusted, but whom you have neglected.

But there are other scenes more dreadful still. The faithless parent must meet his ruined children at the day of judgment, before the bar of God. Fearful will be the interview; and to us, now, utterly inconceivable. No imagination can pourtray the scene, and I attempt it not. And then, eternity, oh! eternity!—who shall bring out from the secrets of that impenetrable state, the condition of children, lost in some measure through the neglect of their parents; and the condition of parents, hearing through everlasting ages the imprecation and reproaches of their own offspring, and all these imprecations and reproaches echoed back from their own conscience. But the picture is too appalling—and if the mere anticipation chills with horror, what must be its reality.

Look for a few moments at a *brighter* scene, and anticipate the meeting, at the judgment day, of pious parents and children, reclaimed, converted, saved by the blessing of God upon their affectionate solicitude, and judicious and persevering efforts for their eternal welfare: but this is as much too bright for the imagination, as the other is too terrific. It is glory, honour, and felicity too great to be imagined. And beyond all this, everlasting ages remain for the child to be blessed with salvation, and the parent to be blessed with the consciousness of having been the happy instrument of eternal blessedness to his offspring.

CHAPTER VI.

THE DUTIES OF CHILDREN TO THEIR PARENTS.

"Children, obey your parents in the Lord; for this is right. Honour thy father and mother; which is the first commandment with promise; that it may be well with thee, and that thou mayest live long on the earth."
EPHES. vi. 1, 2, 3.

"My son keep thy father's commandment, and forsake not the law of thy mother; bind them continually upon thine heart, and tie them about thy neck. When thou goest it shall lead thee; when thou sleepest it shall keep thee; and when thou awakest it shall talk with thee."
PROVERBS vi. 20—22.

"The father of the righteous shall greatly rejoice; and he that begetteth a wise child shall have joy of him. Thy father and thy mother shall be glad, and she that bare thee shall rejoice."
PROVERBS xxiii. 24, 25.

PERHAPS there is no duty the obligations of which are more generally acknowledged than filial piety; none which in the performance yields greater pleasure, nor which, if neglected brings a more severe or righteous retribution. All nations, however sunk in barbarism or elevated by science, have admitted the strength and justice of parental claims, and the unhappy youth who resists them, stands convicted, condemned and reprobated before the tribunal of the world. On the other hand, an eminently dutiful child is an object of delight, admiration and esteem, to all who have an opportunity of witnessing his conduct; he goes through society surrounded by a glory purer than that of fame, and far more conducive to his own comfort; he is a blessing to his parents, and is blessed himself. Children, may all of you be such: and for that purpose, I ask your fixed attention to the statement of your duties, as set before you in this chapter. The obligations of social life are reciprocal. If your parents owe to you all that I have enjoined upon *them*, how much do you owe to your parents? I have been your advocate with *them*, I now become theirs with *you*.

Consider well the relation you sustain to your parents. There is a *natural* connexion between you, inasmuch as they are the instruments of your very existence: a circumstance which of itself seems to invest them, as I have already said, with an almost absolute authority over you. The commonness, the universality of the tie, takes off the mind from contemplating its closeness, its tenderness its sanctity. You are literally parts of themselves, and cannot dwell for a moment upon your descent, without being struck, one should think, with the amazing and solemn weight of obligation that rests upon you towards a father and a mother. But consider, there is not only a natural, but in reference to duty, an *instituted* connexion between you; Jehovah himself has interposed, and uniting the language of revelation with the dictates of reason; the force of authority, to the impulse of nature;

has called you to filial piety, not only as a matter of feeling, but of principle. Study then the relationship, look narrowly and seriously at the connexion subsisting between you. Weigh well the import of the word Parent; think how much is employed in it towards its appropriate object, how many offices it contains in itself,—guardian, ruler, teacher, guide, benefactor, provider: WHAT THEN MUST BE THE OBLIGATIONS OF A CHILD?

The following is a brief summary of filial duties:—

1. You ought to love your parents.

Love is the only state of mind from which all the other duties that you owe them can arise. By love, we mean complacency; and surely this is due to a father and mother. The very relation in which you stand to them demands this. If you are destitute of this, if you are without any propensity of heart towards them, you are in a strange and guilty state of mind. Till you are married, or are in prospect of it, they ought, in most cases, to be the supreme objects of your earthly affections. It is not enough for you to be respectful and obedient, and even kind; but, where there exists no reasons for alienating your heart, you should be *fond* of them. It is of infinite importance that you should watch over the internal state of your mind, and not suffer dislike, alienation, or indifference, to extinguish your regards. Do not take up a prejudice against them, nor allow an unfavourable impression to be made upon your mind. Respect and obedience, if they do not spring from love, are valueless in their nature, and very precarious in their existence.

If you love them, *you will delight to be in their company,* and take pleasure in being at home with them. It is painful to them to see that you are happier any where than at home, and fonder of any other society than theirs. No companion should be so valued by you as a kind father or mother.

If you love them, *you will strive in all things to please them.* We are always anxious to please those whom we regard, and to avoid whatever would give them pain. If we are careless whether we please or displease any one, it is obviously impossible that we can have any affection for them. The essence of piety towards God is a deep solicitude to please him; and the essence of filial piety, is a solicitude to please your parents. Young people, dwell upon this single simple thought, A CHILD'S PLEASURE SHOULD BE TO PLEASE HIS PARENTS. This is love, and the sum of all your duty. If you would adopt this rule, if you would write this upon your heart, if you would make this the standard of your conduct, I might lay down my pen, for it includes every thing in itself. O that you could be brought to reason and to resolve thus:—" I am bound by every tie of God and man, of reason and revelation, of honour and gratitude, to do all I can to make my parents happy, by doing whatever will give them pleasure, and by avoiding whatever will give them pain. By God's help, I will from this hour study and do whatever will promote their comfort. I will make my will to consist in doing theirs, and my earthly happiness to arise from making them happy. I will sacrifice my own predilections, and be satisfied with *their* choice." Noble resolution, and just and proper ! Adopt it, act upon it, and you will never repent of it. Do not have any earthly happiness that is enjoyed at the expence of theirs.

If you love them, *you will desire their good opinion.* We naturally value the esteem of those to whom we are attached : we wish to be thought highly of by them ; and if we are quite careless about their respect for us, it is a sure sign we have no regard for them. Children should be desirous and even anxious to stand high in the opinion of their parents ; and nothing can be a more decisive proof of a bad disposition in a son or a daughter, than their being quite indifferent what their parents think of them. All love must be gone in such a case as this, and the youth is in the road to rebellion and destruction: commendation has lost its value, censure its efficacy, and punishment its power.

2. REVERENCE is the next duty.

" *Honour,*" saith the commandment, " thy father and mother." This reverence has respect to your *feelings*, your *words*, and your *actions*. It consists in part of an inward consciousness of their superiority, and an endeavour to cherish a reverential frame of mind towards them, as placed by God over you. There must be high thoughts of their superiority, both natural and instituted, and a submission of the *heart* to their authority, in a way of sincere and profound respect. Even your love must be that which is exercised and expressed towards a superior. If there be no reverence of the heart, it cannot be expected in the conduct. In all virtue, whether it be that higher kind which has respect to God, or that secondary kind, which relates to our fellow creatures, we must have a right state of heart; for without this, virtue does not exist.

Your *words* should correspond with the reverential feelings of the heart. When speaking *to* them, your address, both in language and in tones, should be modest, submissive, and respectful; not loud, boisterous, impertinent, or even familiar: for they are not your equals, but your superiors. If at any time you differ from them in opinion, your views should be expressed, not with the flippancy and pertinaciousness of disputants, but with the meek inquisitiveness of pupils. Should they reprove and even more sharply than you think is due, you must lay your hand upon your mouth, and neither answer them again, nor shew resentment. Your reverence for them should be so great, as to impose a considerable restraint upon your speech in their company; for much is due to the presence of a parent. It is exceedingly offensive to hear a pert, clamorous, talkative young person, unchecked by the countenance of a father or mother, and engaging much of the conversation of a party to himself. Young persons should always be modest and retiring in company, but more especially when their parents are there. You should also be careful about the manner of speaking *of* them *to others*. You should never talk of their faults, for this is like Ham's uncovering the nakedness of his father. You must not speak of them in a jocose or familiar manner, nor say any thing that would lead others to think lightly, or to suppose that *you* thought lightly of them. If they are attacked in their reputation, you are with promptitude and firmness, though with meekness, to defend them, so far as truth will allow; and even if the charge be true, to make all the excuses that veracity will permit, and protest against the cruelty of degrading your parents in your presence.

Reverence should extend to all your *behaviour* towards your parents. In all your conduct towards them, give them the greatest honour; let it be observed by others that you pay them all possible respect, and let it also be seen by themselves, when there is no spectator near. Your conduct should always be under restraint, when they are within sight; not the restraint of dread, but of esteem. How would you act if the king were in the room? Would you be as free, as familiar, as noisy, as when he had retired, or before he had entered? I am of opinion, that parents let down their dignity, and undermine their authority, by allowing the same rude and boisterous behaviour in their presence, as in their absence. This should not be. When reason is expanding in children, they should be made to understand and feel the truth of what I have already affirmed, that there is an outward respect due to the very presence of a parent. All rude and noisy rushing in and out of a father or mother's company is unmeet. It is the etiquette of our court, that no one shall enter the royal presence, when the king is upon his throne, without obeisance; nor in retiring, turn his back upon the throne. I do not ask for the same obsequiousness in families, but I ask for the principle from which it arises, a respectful deference for authority.

3. The next duty is OBEDIENCE.

"Children *obey* your parents," says the apostle in his epistle to the Colossians. This is one of the most obvious dictates of nature; even the irrational creatures are obedient by instinct, and follow the signs of the parent beast, or bird, or reptile. Perhaps there is no duty more generally acknowledged than this. Your obedience should *begin early;* the younger you are, the more you need a guide and a ruler. It should be *universal:* "Children obey your parents," said the apostle, "in all things." The only exception to this, is when their commands are, in the letter or spirit of them, opposed to the commands of God. In this case, as well as in every other, we must obey God, rather than man. But even here your refusal to comply with the sinful injunction of a parent, must be uttered in a meek and respectful manner, so that it shall be manifest you are actuated by pure, conscientious motives, and not by a mere rebellious resistance of parental authority. Your obedience should have no other exception than that which is made by conscience: in your situation, inclination and taste are out of the question, both must be crossed, opposed, and set aside when opposed to parental authority. Obedience should be *prompt.* As soon as the command is uttered, it should be complied with. It is a disgrace to any child that it should be necessary for a father or a mother to repeat a command. You should even anticipate, if possible their injunctions, and not wait till their will is announced in words. A tardy obedience loses all its glory. It should be *cheerful*. A reluctant virtue is no virtue at all. Constrained and unwilling obedience, is rebellion in *principle*; it is vice clothed in the garment of holiness. God loveth a cheerful giver, and so does man. A child retiring from a parent's presence, muttering, sullen, and murmuring, is one of the ugliest spectacles in creation: of what value is any thing he does, in such a temper as this? It should be *self-denying*. You must give up your own wills, and sacrifice your own predilections, and perform the things that are difficult, as well as those that are easy. When a soldier receives a command, although he may be at home in comfort, and he is required at once to go into the field of danger, he hesitates not, he considers he has no option. A child has no more room for the gratification of self-will than the soldier has; he *must* obey. It should be *uniform*. Filial obedience is generally rendered without much difficulty when the parents are present, but not always with the same unreservedness, when they are absent. Young people, you should despise the meanness, and abhor the wickedness, of consulting the wishes, and obeying the injunctions of your parents, only when they are there to witness your conduct. Such hypocrisy is detestable. Act upon nobler principles. Let it be enough for you to know what is the will of a parent, to ensure obedience, even though continents laid, and oceans rolled between you and your father. Carry this injunction with you every where; let the voice of conscience be to you, instead of *his* voice, and the consciousness that God sees you be enough to ensure your immediate compliance. How sublimely simple and striking was the reply of the child, who upon being pressed in company to take something which his absent parents had forbidden him to touch ; and who, upon being reminded tha they were not there to witness him, replied, " very true, but God and my conscience are here." Be it your determination, to imitate this beautiful example of filial piety, and obey in all things even your *absent* parents.

4. Submission to the family discipline and rule is no less your duty than obedience to commands.

In every well ordered family there is a rule of government; there is subordination, system, discipline, reward, and punishment; and to these, *all* the children must be in subjection. Submission requires, that if at any time you have behaved so as to render parental chastisement necessary, you should take it patiently, and not be infuriated by passion, or excited to resistance. Remember that your parents are commanded by God to correct your faults, that they are actuated by love in performing this self-denying duty, and that it costs them more pain to inflict it, than it does you to endure it. Ingenuously confess your faults, and submit to whatever punishment their authority and wisdom may appoint. One of the loveliest sights in the domestic economy, next to that of a uniformly obedient child, is a disobedient one brought to a right sense of his misconduct, and quietly submitting to the penalty he has incurred. It is a proof both of strength of mind and of good disposition of heart, to say, " I have done wrong, and it is meet I should bear chastisement."

In the case of elder children, all other correction than that of rebuke, and the expression by language of parental displeasure, is of course out of the question; but where this is necessary, such young persons as have merited it, should exercise profound submission. It is exceedingly painful when a parent, in addition to the extreme pain which it costs him to administer reproof to such children, has to endure the anguish produced by their utter indifference, smiling contempt, sullen murmuring, or insolent replies. This conduct is the more guilty, because the authors of it are arrived at an age when they may be supposed to have advanced so far in the growth of their understanding, as to perceive how deeply laid are the foundations of the parental authority, in nature, reason, and revelation, and how necessary it is that the reins of parental discipline should not be relaxed. If then, you have committed one error in deserving reproof, do not commit another in resenting it. Keep all still within, let not your passions rebel against your judgment, but suppress in a moment the rising tumult of the soul. The conduct of some children after reproof, is a deeper wound on the heart of a parent, than that which preceded and deserved the reproof. On the other hand, I know not a greater mark of nobleness of mind, nor any thing which tends to raise a young person higher in the esteem of a parent, or to endear him more to a father's heart, than a humble submission to reproof, and an ingenuous confession of his fault. A friend of mine had a son, long since gone to join the immortals, who, having one day displeased his father before his younger brothers and sisters, not only meekly submitted to parental rebuke, but when the family were assembled at the dinner table, rose before them all, and after having confessed his fault, and craved his father's forgiveness, admonished the junior branches of the family to take warning by his example, and be cautious never to distress their parents, whom they were under such obligations to love and respect. Nothing could be more lovely or more impressive, than this noble act. He rose, by his apology, to a higher place in the regard and esteem of his parents and the family, than he occupied even before his fault. Sullenness, impertinence, and obstinate resistance, are meanness, cowardice, littleness, compared with such an action as this, which combines an heroic magnanimity with the profoundest humility.

Subjection requires also, *a due observance of the rules laid down for the maintenance of family order.* In every well ordered family, things are not left to chance, but regulated by fixed laws; there is a time for every thing and every thing in its time; a place for every thing and every thing in its place. Meals, prayer, going to bed, and rising in the morning, are all in their appointed season. To these rules it is the obvious duty of every branch of the family to submit. The sons and daughters may be growing up or arrived at full age; this matters not, they must submit to the law of the house, and their age is an additional reason for their submission, as it supposes a maturity of judgment, which enables them to perceive more clearly the grounds of all moral obligation. They may think the rules too strict; but if the parent has enacted them, they should be in subjection, and that, as long as they continue members of the little community, though it be almost to old age. It is for the parent to decide also what *visitors* shall be brought to the house: and it is in the highest degree unbecoming for a child to introduce, or even wish to attempt to introduce, any companion, contrary to the known will of a parent. The same remark will apply to *recreations;* parents must determine this point, and no child that has the proper feelings of a child, would desire to set up any amusements that the taste, and especially that the conscience of a father or mother forbids. Instances have occurred of young people inviting such friends, and joining with them in such diversions, in the absence of their parents, as they know to be decidedly contrary to the law of the house. This is such an act of base and wicked rebellion against parental authority, and such an unprincipled disregard to parental comfort, as language is too weak to characterize. Even the *books* which are brought into the house must be in accordance with the domestic rule. If the parent forbid the introduction of novels, romances, or any other books, a child in most cases should forego his own predilections, and yield to an authority which he cannot resist without opposing the institute of nature and religion.

5. It is the duty of children TO CONSULT THEIR PARENTS.

They are the guides of your youth; your natural counsellors; the family oracle, which you are ever to consult, and the responses of which are to be received with pious reverence. Even if you have just reason to suspect the solidity and penetration of their judgment, it is due to the relation in which you stand to them, to undertake nothing without laying the matter before them, and obtaining their opinion. How much more ready should you be to do this, where you have every reason to confide in their wisdom. You are young and inexperienced; the path of life is in a considerable degree untrodden by you, and contingencies are perpetually arising, which you have yet acquired no experience to understand, and to turn to account. They have travelled the road, and know its turnings, its dangers, and its difficulties. Go to your parents, then, with every affair; consult them on the subject of companions, books, recreations. Let a father's and a mother's ear be the receptacle of all your cares. Have no secrets which you conceal from them. Especially consult with them on the subjects of *trade* and *marriage*. On the former, you perhaps need their pecuniary assistance, and how can you expect this if you take not their advice, as to the best way of employing *their* property. As to marriage, I need not repeat at any length what I have already said on this subject. The scripture has furnished us with many fine instances of the deference paid in patriarchal times by children to their parents. Isaac and Jacob both appear to have left the selection of their wives to their parents. Ruth, though a daughter in law, was willing to be guided entirely by Naomi. Ishmael asked his mother's advice; and Sampson sought for his parent's consent. The simplicity of that age has departed, and in the advance of society, more of the power of selection now vests in the children; but it should not be exercised independently of parental advice. An old divine said thus to his sons :—" When you are youths, choose your callings, when men, choose your wives, only take me along with you; it may be, old men see farther than you." Another ancient writer has this remark ;—" It may be considered, that parents who brought forth and bred up their children, should by no means be bereft of them, without their consent; and since they are so much their goods and possessions, it were a kind of purloining to give themselves away without their parents' leave." And on this subject, a heathen may teach many who profess to be christians; for Cyrus, on being invited to form a connexion with a particular individual, replied, " I like the lady, her dowry, and family; but I must have these agree with my parents' will, and then I will marry her."

6. IMITATE THE GOOD EXAMPLE of your parents.

I say their *good* example, for if they unhappily set you a *bad* one, it is at the peril of your soul that you follow it. It was a noble answer which Frederick IV. Elector Palatine of the Rhine, returned to the prince, who advised him to follow the example of his father Lewis:—" In the business o religion we must follow the example of parents and ancestors, only so far as they are agreeable to the will of God." Marcus Aurelius Antonius, when he came to the throne of Imperial Rome, publicly expressed his determination not to follow the usual conduct of the Cæsars, but to act as a disciple of the pious Antonine, and to act, and speak, and think, as his foster-father did. Survey the conduct of *your* parents; let their failings be thrown back in shadow, their excellences brought out in full relief. Where they are truly pious, be followers of their religious character. You bear the likeness of their bodies, receive also the impress of their minds. Seek to catch the family feature of their piety. A wicked child, of godly parents, is the most awful character upon earth. With what horror do I look upon such an one! That *he* should swear, who was taught to pray! That *he* should violate the Sabbath, who was led up from his infantine days, to the house of God! That *he* should despise religion, who has ever seen its beautiful form, in the example of a godly father, and a pious mother! That *he* should be a friend of profane and unclean persons, who from a child has been the companion of saints! Shocking spectacle!! But even where there may be no actual irreligion, there is oftentimes a want of true religion; and this also, is distressing. What an aggravation is it to the sin of being without piety, to have lived all the earlier part of life, with an example of true godliness before our eyes! This is a dreadful and actual resistance of the most alluring means which heaven ever employs for the conversion of a sinner; it is a resolute determination to neglect and forget religion, in spite of an interesting and powerful memorial of it constantly before your eyes. What a meeting will such children have with their parents at the last day!!

7. The last duty I shall mention is KINDNESS.

This should extend through the whole of your deportment; but there are several cases in which it will have a more enlarged opportunity for displaying its beauty, and exerting its energy.

When parents are *greatly inferior in talents and acquirements*, it is a fine occasion for the exercise of filial piety. We know instances in which the father and mother are lamentably deficient, not only in information, but in judgment: their weakness is manifest to all, and cannot be concealed from their family; by whom, indeed, the sad effects of their imbecility are daily felt and deplored. Here then is an opportunity for a display of noble and exalted kindness, on the part of children. Young people, if you are placed in such circumstances, endeavour constantly to remember that notwithstanding all their weakness, they are your parents still, and hold a parent's claim. Never, never taunt them with their defects, for this is cruelty in the extreme; but on the contrary, strive to the uttermost to prevent them from suffering any painful consciousness of their inferiority. Do not laugh at their mistakes, nor ever suffer yourselves so to expose or to correct them, as to wound their feelings. If they are obstinate, yield to them ; if irritable, bear with them : and when they show their incapacity for governing with wisdom, instead of snatching the sceptre from their hand, insensibly assist them to wield it with greater propriety. It is a beautiful sight to behold a fine, intelligent, strong-minded son or daughter, straining every nerve, and employing every faculty to endure and conceal the faults of such a parent, and to throw an air of respectability over one, that has no respectability of his own.

" There is often, especially in the middle classes of life, as great a difference of mental culture in the parent and the child, as if they had lived at the distance of many centuries. The wealth that has been acquired by patient industry or some fortunate adventure, may be employed in diffusing all the refinements of science and literature to the children of those to whom the very words, science and literature, are words of which they would scarcely be able, even with the help of a dictionary, to understand the meaning. In a rank of life still lower, there are not wanting many meritorious individuals, who, uninstructed themselves, labour indefatigably to obtain the means of liberal instruction or one, whose wisdom in after years, where he is to astonish the village, may gratify at once their ambition and love. It would indeed, be painful to think, that any one, whose superiority of knowledge has cost his parents so much fatigue, and so many privations of comforts, which, but for the expense of the means of his acquired superiority, they might have enjoyed, should turn against them, in his own mind, the acquirements which were to them of so costly a purchase, despising them for the very ignorance which gave greater merit to their sacrifice, and proud of a wisdom far less noble, when it can thus feel contempt, than the humble ignorance which it despises."

Kindness will shew itself *in generous attention to* POOR *parents.* In the revolution of this world, and by the vicissitudes of human affairs, many children have left their parents behind them in the humble vale of poverty, and some have lost their filial piety in the ascent. Few more shocking scenes can be presented to a feeling mind, than a rich son or daughter ashamed of, and unkind to, his poor father or mother. Such wretches deserve the fate of the proud monarch of Babylon, and would have no more than their desert if they were driven from the company of men to herd with beasts, to which they are more allied in disposition than to human beings. How beautiful a scene, the very opposite of that which I have just considered, was exhibited in the palace of Pharaoh, when Joseph, then the Prime Minister of the state, led in a poor old shepherd to the presence of the king, and before all the lords of the Egyptian court, introduced the decrepid and care-worn pilgrim as his father. Who, after looking at this, will ever be ashamed of a parent because he is clad in the garb of poverty? What a halo of glory did that one act draw round the honoured brow of Joseph; the lustre of the golden chain that hung from his neck was dim compared with the brightness of this action, and the chariot in which he rode with almost imperial pomp before the people, raised him not to so high an eminence, as that which he occupied, when he stood before the monarch with the patriarch of Canaan leaning on his arm. Never be ashamed of your parents then, because of their poverty.

Let your kindness operate *in the way of affording them all things necessary for their comfort.* The author of the Æneid has denominated his hero the pious Æneas, because of the heroic manner in which he bore his decrepid father from the flames of Troy. Two inhabitants of Sicily obtained a celebrity in antient story for their kindness to their aged parents in carrying them upon their shoulders from an irruption of Mount Etna.

We have another instance of modern times. " Mr. Robert Tillotson went up to London on a visit to his son, then Dean of Canterbury, and being in the dress of a plain countryman was insulted by one of the Dean's servants, for enquiring if *John Tillotson* was at home. His person, however, being described to the Dean, he immediately exclaimed, " It is my worthy father :" and running down to the door to receive him, he fell down upon his kness in the presence of his servants, to ask his father's blessing."

And how have the poet, the historian, and the painter loved to exhibit that beautiful picture of filial piety, first given by Pliny, of a daughter, who, when her mother was condemned to be starved to death, obtained leave from the keeper to visit the prison daily, and there nourished her parent from her own breast. A similar occurrence took place afterwards, in which a daughter nourished her father in the same manner; the action was considered so striking, that it obtained the honourable appellation of *The Roman Charity.* The senate decreed that the father should be restored to his child, and that on the spot where the prison stood, a temple should be erected to FILIAL PIETY.

There are however, few instances of more touching kindness to parents, than that mentioned by Mr. Bruce, in his Juvenile Anecdotes.—

" An officer having remained some time at Kingston, in Surrey, for the purpose of raising recruits, received orders to join his regiment. On the evening before his departure, a YOUNG MAN of the most engaging aspect made his appearance, and desired to be enlisted into his company. His air at once indicated a well cultivated mind, and commanded respect.

" He betrayed, however, evident marks of perturbation, and was greatly embarrassed; the officer asked the cause of it: ' I tremble, said he, lest you should deny my request.' Whilst he was speaking, the tears rolled down his cheeks. ' No,' answered the officer " I accept your offer most heartily ; but why should you imagine a refusal ?' ' Because the bounty which I expect may perhaps be too high.' ' How much then do you demand?' said the officer. ' It is no unworthy motive, but an urgent claim, that compels me to ask ten guineas; and I shall be the most miserable of mankind if you refuse me.' ' Ten guineas!' said the officer, ' that indeed is very high: but I am pleased with you; I trust to your honour for the discharge of your duty, and will strike the bargain at once. Here are ten guineas: to morrow we depart.'

"The young man, overwhelmed with joy, begged permission to return home, to perform a sacred duty, and promised to be back within an hour. The officer, impressed by the honesty of his countenance, yielded to his desire; but observing something mysterious in his manner, he was induced, by curiosity, to follow him at some distance. He saw him hastening towards the town prison, where he knocked and was admitted. The officer quickened his pace; and when he came to the door of the prison, he overheard the young man say to the jailor: ' Here is the money for which my father is imprisoned; I put it into your hands, and I request you will conduct me to him immediately, that I may release him from his misery.' The jailor did as he requested.

"The officer delayed a few minutes, that the young man might have an opportunity of being alone with his father: he then followed him. What a scene! he saw the son in the arms of a venerable and aged father, who, without uttering a word, pressed him to his heart, and bedewed him with tears. A few minutes passed before he observed the officer, who, deeply affected, approached them, and said to the old man,— 'Compose yourself, I will not deprive you of so worthy a son. Permit me to restore him to you, that I may not regret the money which he has employed in so virtuous a manner.'

"The father and son fell upon their knees at his feet. The young man refused, at first, to accept of his proffered freedom: but the worthy officer insisted that he should remain with his father. He accompanied them both from the prison, and took his leave with the pleasing reflection of having contributed to the happiness of a worthy son and an unfortunate father."

What mind is not enamoured, what heart is not affected, by such touching instances of filial kindness. And what child is not ready to exclaim, "O my father, my mother, I will share with you my last crust, and feel at once both honoured and happy, to return upon you, in your old age, the kindness you bestowed upon me in my youth, childhood, and infancy."

Kindness will manifest itself by *affectionate attention* and *tender sympathy, in their sickness.* I do not know where in all our world to find a lovelier, holier, sweeter scene, than that of a pious and affectionate daughter, devoting her time, and strength, and inventive assiduities, to the comfort of a mother or a father confined for years to the room and the bed of sickness. Such children I have known; and ineffably admired: who, at an age when there is usually a taste and capacity for the pleasures of society, have abstracted themselves from all company, to be the constant and almost sole companion of that dear sufferer, to alleviate whose sorrows was their only happiness. Scarcely have they permitted themselves to walk abroad and enjoy the scenes of nature, even to recruit their wasting strength and prepare for fresh activities in the sick chamber, lest in their absence a pang should be felt which none could so well mitigate as they, or a want endured which they could best supply. I knew one such, who had a sick father lived much longer, would have preceded him to the grave, and died a martyr to filial piety. Nothing could ever tempt her away from his side by day, and not often did a night pass without her stealing quietly to the chamber door, at which unconscious of the frost which was assailing her delicate frame, she stood listening to ascertain if all was still, not daring to enter, lest she should disturb that slumber which perhaps he was enjoying. I remember in another case, visiting a cottage, in which a sick man lay dying, who had been long ill; his wife was ministering to his comfort, and in one corner of the room, there was a girl of twelve years of age busily employed at her needle. On my asking how they were supported in their affliction, the mother replied, "principally, sir, by that child's work; she is up every morning at four o'clock, and is diligently employed till late at night; she cheerfully bears all this labour, and gives its produce to sustain us." Young people, read and ponder these interesting details, and imitate these beautiful examples. Put forth all your tenderness, shrink from no self-denial; endure, not only without murmuring, but with cheerfulness, any sacrifices to comfort a sick parent. Aspire to the character of being a ministering angel to a father or mother. Let them see that you account it no hardship, but a felicity to wait upon them. It is in your power to alleviate or aggravate to an inconceivable degree their sufferings, according as you are kind or unkind. Covet the testimony which many a one has received, when the sufferer has said, with tears in her eyes, "that dear child is my companion, my friend, my nurse, and all my earthly delight." O what is the concord of sweet sounds at the concert?—what the gay and glittering attractions of the ball-room?—what the dazzling scenes of the theatre?—or to come to more lawful enjoyments—what the exhiliration of the public meeting, compared with the consciousness of having smoothed the bed of sickness, and alleviated the sufferings of disease, for an afflicted parent. If the conscience of any that shall read these pages shall reproach them for neglect:—if they know that they have heard their parents mildly reprove them for their want of sympathy, let them consider what must be the anguish of those parents' hearts, who have to say in the bitterness of their soul, to their own children, "Is it nothing to you, all ye that pass by, come, see if there was ever sorrow like unto my sorrow;" and who, disappointed in the hope of tenderness from their own offspring, turn for help to their neighbours; and taking up the piteous complaint of Job, say, "Pity me, pity me, O my *friends,* for the hand of God hath touched me." Unfeeling youth, your neglect will one day find you out, and at some future time may be, perhaps, returned upon you by the cruel conduct of your own children.

Kindness will often be put to a severe test, *by the bad temper,* or *the stern and tyrannical government* of parents. It is difficult, I know, to be kind to those who are unkind to us; but it is our duty in all cases, much more to a parent. Nothing must allow you to be otherwise than the dutiful, affectionate child. No ebullitions of passion, no manifestation of unreasonable discontent, no caprice, no unmerited reproach on their part, should throw you off your guard. It may be sometimes necessary to remonstrate, but never can be proper to return railing for railing. Kindness may do more, in such circumstances, to soften and remove the evil, than angry resistance;—" A soft answer turneth away wrath."

"Lovely as virtue is," says Dr. Brown, " in all its forms, there is no form in which it is more lovely, than in the tender ministry of offices of kindness: where the kindness, perhaps, is scarcely felt, or considered less as kindness, than as the duty which might have been fairly demanded, and which there is no merit, therefore, in having paid. Though we have often the gratification of seeing, in the progress of life, many beautiful examples of age, that is not more venerable for its past virtues, than amiable, with a lasting and still increasing gentleness, which softens the veneration indeed, but augments it even while it softens it, it is not always that the last years of life present to us this delightful aspect; and when the temper is, in these last years, unfortunately clouded,—when there is no smile of kindness in the faded eye, that grows bright again for moments only when there is fretfulness in the heart,—when the voice that is feeble, only in the utterance of grateful regard, is still sometimes loud with tones of a very different expression,—the kindness, which, in its unremitting attention, never shows by a word or look, the sadness that is felt on these undeserved reproaches, and that regards them only as proofs of a weakness that requires still more to be comforted, is a kindness which virtue alone can inspire and animate, but which, in the bosom that is capable of it, virtue must already have well rewarded. How delightful is the spectacle, when amid all the temptation of youth and beauty, we witness some gentle heart, that gives to the couch of the feeble, and perhaps of the thankless and repining, those hours which others find too short for the successive gaieties with which an evening can be filled, and that prefers to the smile of universal admiration, the single smile of enjoyment, which, after many vain efforts has at last been kindled on one solitary cheek!"

Another circumstance remains to be mentioned, which will render it extremely difficult, sometimes, to be at once obedient to God, and to your parents;— difficult to manifest all the kindness which they may expect, and at the same time, to regard the dictates of conscience; I mean, where the children are pious, and the parents *are still in an unconverted state.* This is no uncommon case, and always a trying one wherever it occurs. Those who are placed in such a situation, need much wisdom and much grace to conduct themselves with propriety, so as to give no unnecessary pain to their parents, and yet at the same time, to maintain their consistency as christians. To young persons in such circumstances, I say, let there be deep and unaffected humility; no spiritual pride, no apparent consciousness of moral superiority, no saying, "stand by, I am holier than thou;" nothing approaching, in the most distant manner, to contempt of your parents, on account of their state. When it is necessary, as it sometimes may be, to oppose their wishes and refuse their requests, because they interfere with your duty to God, let your dissent not assume the shape of disobedience to them, let it be expressed in a mild and respectful manner, and be made obviously to appear to be the result of conscientious motives, and not of caprice, or any want of right feeling towards them. In all other things, in which religion is not concerned, let there be additional effort and ingenuity to please them, so that they may have nothing against you, but as touching the law of your God. It may be sometimes necessary for you to *express* the solicitude which you ought always to *feel* for their spiritual welfare; you must then be careful to avoid the appearance of dictation, lecturing, and reproach, and address yourselves to them in a humble and prudent manner. You should put suitable books in their way; and if they are not in the habit of hearing the gospel preached, you may invite them to hear the joyful sound. With all this, you must take especial pains, that your own religion may be consistent and practical; visible in all your conduct, and more particularly conspicuous, in the kind, and tender, and dutiful manner, in which you discharge your obligations to them.

Such is a compendium of filial duties. Let children read them, study them, sincerely desire to perform them, and pray to Almighty God for the grace that is in Christ Jesus, to assist them in discharging their obligations.

Many and cogent MOTIVES may be brought forward to enforce the performance of these duties.

Observe the manner in which they are enjoined in scripture. Perhaps there are few branches of moral obligation more frequently alluded to, or more variously enjoined, than that of filial piety. The lives of the Patriarchs, from the beginning of the world, are so drawn up as to exhibit and recommend this virtue. It is commanded in one of the precepts of the *Moral law.* By the ceremonial law, stubborn disobedience to parental authority was punished with death. The book of Proverbs contains almost innumerable apothegms on this subject. The prophets very frequently allude to it: and Jeremiah, in the history of the Rechabites, has preserved a very extraordinary instance of hereditary filial obedience, perpetuated through a period, which, in the time of that prophet, had lasted three centuries, and which was rewarded by the following testimony and promise of the Lord:—" Thus saith Jehovah of Hosts, the God of Israel; because ye have obeyed the commandment of Jonadab, your father, and kept all his precepts, and done according to all that he hath commanded you; therefore, thus saith Jehovah of Hosts, the God of Israel; Jonadab, the son of Rechab, shall not want a man to stand before me for ever." If we come forward to the New Testament, we find it again and again brought into view. We see it embodied and enforced in the example of Christ; of whom it is said, Jesus went down and was subject unto his parents. Yes, in the matchless constellation of perfect moral excellences that formed his character, and are presented for our admiration and imitation, one bright and beauteous star is filial piety. Fix, young people, your eye upon that star, so mildly beaming, and so radiantly shining, as an example for you. That wonderful personage, GOD MANIFEST IN THE FLESH, was subject, we have reason to believe, to his parents, till at the age of thirty he entered upon his public ministry; and those parents, be it remembered, were a poor but pious couple, who earned their daily bread by the sweat of their brow. With them he dwelt, in their humble abode, and laboured, in all probability, for their support. And even amidst the agonies of the cross, neither his own personal suffering, nor the sublime and glorious scenes connected with the redemption of a world, abstracted his thoughts and solicitude from the mother of his human nature; and even then did filial piety shine forth, a bright speck still visible upon the orb of glory, which was rising upon the world. The apostles enforced it by various commendations. " Children, obey your parents," says Paul in one place, "*for it is right;*" a thing not obligatory merely because it is commanded, but commanded because it is right; not a mere positive institute, but wholly moral; a duty enjoined not only by revelation, but by reason; one of the first lessons taught by nature to a rational creature. So right and proper is it, that all nations, antient and modern, civilized and savage, admit its obligations. In another place, it is declared to be " well pleasing unto the Lord." It is that in which he delights, because it is the very disposition towards himself which he requires. And then, in his catalogue of dark deeds, and horrid dispositions, and atrocious characters, the apostle places disobedience to parents. The loud, strong voice of revelation is lifted to proclaim over the surface of the globe, " Children obey your parents, and honour your father and mother; *for this is well pleasing to the Lord:*" while the voice of nature echoes back the command, "Children, obey your parents, *for this is right.*"

A child of any degree of generosity will be influenced to obey his parents, *by a consideration of their comfort.*

The earthly happiness of a father and a mother, depends far more upon the conduct of their children, than upon any thing else. Their trade may prosper, their wealth accumulate; they may dwell amidst every kind of luxury and splendour, in the most beautiful spot which creation can present, yet an undutiful child may, by his disobedience and unkindness, throw a dark and chilling shadow over all, and envelope every thing in gloom. On the other hand, affectionate and obedient children supply the lack of riches, soften the weight of care, sweeten the cup of affliction, and shed a pleasing light over what would be otherwise a dark and dreary scene of human woe. Children have their parents' happiness in their keeping. They stand at the fountains of our earthly destiny, and send into our dwelling the waters of bitterness or of sweetness, as their conduct towards us shall be dutiful or unkind. They cannot know, till experience shall teach them, the trembling and exquisite sensitiveness of our hearts, and how slight a puncture draws the life's blood of our peace. So true it is, as was said by the wise man, that "a foolish son is the heaviness of his mother," aye, and of his father too; he is a spot on their character; a blast upon their hopes: a nuisance to their family; and a thorn in their hearts.

Nearly connected with this, as another motive, is *gratitude.* No child can know, till he becomes a parent himself, what he owes to *his* parents; and not then till he has added all the cares, and toils, and anxieties which are excited by the child, the boy, the youth, the man, in addition to those which are awakened by the *infant of days.* Parental solicitude is, of course, produced by the first sight of the child; but the infancy of the babe, is but the infancy of our solicitude, which grows with its growth, and strengthens with its strength. Children are ever contracting obligations from the first moment of their existence. What owes not the *babe* to his mother, for that watchfulness, and labour, and anxiety, which scarcely rest by day, or sleep by night. Other animals, though nourished by their parents, are taught many things by instinct; but man, the most helpless of all creatures, must learn every thing from his parents, in the first stage of his existence. Let any one calculate, if he can, the hours of labour, sleeplessness and anxiety; the tears, the tremblings, the alarms, which one weakly infant costs a mother, before he leaves her arms, and stands erect upon his feet in his own strength. My young friend, had your mother remitted her care for one single hour, or ceased, but for a short season, her vigilant inspection, you might have been consumed in your cradle, or have been now a cripple or an idiot. How many months rolled by, before you could wash away a speck of defilement from your frame, help yourself to medicine, or to food, express in articulate language a single want, put on a garment, or defend yourself against an enemy so feeble as a wasp. What then are your obligations to the woman who did all this *for* you, and delighted to do it ? I cannot follow you through the successive stages of your existence, at each of which, you were accumulating fresh obligations to both father and mother, for education, with all its advantages, for instruction in trade, and that capacity you now possess for attaining to respectability in life; but above all, for that ceaseless, and manifest, and earnest solicitude for your eternal happiness, by which you have had the road to glory, honour, and immortality opened to your view, and have been admonished to walk in it! O, sum up, if you can, your obligations to your parents: but you cannot. And can you resist *this* motive to obedience? What, has gratitude perished in your soul, till its very root has died in the soil of your depraved nature? Yes; it must be so, if you are unkind to your parents: you stand proved before the universe, to have nothing of a child, but the name and the mere fleshly relation, which you possess in common with the tiger, or the serpent, or the toad, but you have not the feelings of a child; you are a kind of monstrous production, out of the course of nature, and like all such productions, fill the mind with loathing and horror. Few there are, I hope, that will read these pages, to whom such an expostulation is applicable; on the contrary, many, I believe, will experience as they proceed, the generous emotions of gratitude swelling higher and higher in their bosom, till, with a burst of virtuous feeling, they exclaim, " Accept, my parents, of the surrender, which a sense of my obligation to you compels me to make, of my whole future life, to the promotion of your comfort."

Interest pleads with children for their dutiful behaviour to their parents.

An undutiful child cannot be a *happy* one. Peace

must leave the breast with filial piety, whenever it departs; and uneasiness and misery, and occasional shame and remorse, enter to dwell in the wretched bosom; while the affectionate and dutiful child has a perpetual feast within. And mark the language of the apostle, " Honour thy father and mother ; *which is the first commandment with promise ; that it may be well with thee, and that thou mayest live long on the earth."* This is an allusion, it is true, to the temporal promises of the Sinai Covenant, and perhaps to the law which doomed the disobedient son to be judicially cut off from the people. But yet, as repeated by a *New* Testament writer, it must to a certain extent, be in force still. Dr. Dwight has the following remarks on this passage which deserve consideration. " In conversing with the plain people of this country, distinguished for their good sense, and careful observation of facts, I have found them, to a great extent, firmly persuaded of the verification of this promise in our own times; and ready to produce a variety of proofs from cases, in which they have seen the blessing realized. *Their* opinion is *mine*, and with their experience my own has coincided.

" Indeed no small measure of prosperity seems ordinarily *interwoven* with a course of filial piety. The comfort which it ensures to parents, the harmony which it produces in the family, the peace which it yields in the conscience, are all essential ingredients of happiness. To these it adds the approbation of every beholder, the possession of a fair and lasting reputation, the confidence and good will of every worthy man, and of consequence, an opportunity of easily gaining those useful employments which good men have to give. Beyond this it naturally associates itself with temperance, moderation, and sobriety, which furnish a solid foundation for health and long life. In my own apprehension, however, these are not *all* its blessings. I do not say that miracles are wrought for its reward. Neither will I say that purer gales breathe to preserve its health; nor that softer suns arise, or more timely rains descend, to mature its harvest; nor that more propitious winds blow, to waft its ships home in safety. But I will say, that on the tide of Providence multiplied blessings are borne into its possession, at seasons when they are unexpected, in ways unforeseen, and by means unprovided by its own forecast, which are often of high importance; which, altogether, constitute a rich proportion of prosperity; and which, usually, are not found by persons of the contrary character. At the same time those who act well as children, almost of course, act well as men and women; and thus have taken, without design, the scion of happiness from the parental stock, and grafted it upon other stems, which bear fruit abundantly to themselves. Here, in the language of **Dr. Watts**,

' It revives, and bears,
' A train of blessings for their heirs.'

If motives so forcible and tender as these, have no effect, nothing is left me to do, but to remind the children of disobedience, of that day of judgment, which God hath appointed to judge the world in righteousness, by Jesus Christ, and to give to every one according to the things done in the body whether they are good or bad. " In that most awful season, when the wicked shall see the judge *sit above them*, angry and severe, inexorable and terrible; *under them* an intolerable hell: *within* them their consciences clamorous and diseased; *without them*, all the world on fire; *on the right hand*, those men glorified, whom they persecuted and despised; *on the left hand*, the devils accusing;" then shall it be found that the severest sentence of the Almighty, and the bitterest dregs of the vials of his wrath, will be poured out on the disobedient and ungodly child of those parents who trained him up in the nurture of the Lord.

CHAPTER VII.

ON THE FRATERNAL DUTIES.

"Next in order to the relationship of the parent and the child, may be considered the relation which the child bears to those who are united with him by the same tie, to the same parental bosoms. If friendship be delightful, if it be above all delightful to enjoy the continued friendship of those who are endeared to us by the intimacy of many years, who can discourse with us of the frolics of the school, of the adventures and studies of the college, of the years when we first ranked ourselves with men in the free society of the world, how delightful must be the friendship of those who, accompanying us through all this long period, with a closer union than any casual friend, can go still farther back, from the school to the very nursery, which witnessed our common pastimes; who have had an interest in every event that has related to us, and in every person that excited our love or our hatred; who have honoured with us those to whom we have paid every filial honour in life, and wept with us over those whose death has been to us the most lasting sorrow of our heart. Such in its wide, unbroken sympathy, is the friendship of brothers, considered even as friendship only: and how many circumstances of additional interest does this union receive, from the common relationship to those who have original claims to our still higher regard, and to whom we offer an acceptable service, in extending our affection to those whom they love. In treating of the circumstances that tend peculiarly to strengthen this tie, CICERO extends his view even to the common sepulchre that is at last to enclose us. It is indeed a powerful image, a symbol, and almost a lesson of unanimity. Every dissention of man with man, excites in us a feeling of painful incongruity. But we feel a peculiar incongruity in the discord of those, whom one roof has continued to shelter through life, and whose dust is afterwards to mingle under a single stone."

DR. THOMAS BROWN.

To secure the comfort and well being of a state, it is not only necessary for the sovereign to be wise and patriotic, and the laws justly and impartially administered, but the people must be well affected both towards the government, and towards each other: there must be a tie which binds them to each other, as well as to the state: there must be the fellowship of good neighbourhood. So also the happiness and welfare of a family, depend not exclusively on the conduct of the parents to the children, nor on the conduct of the children to the parents, but also on the conduct of the children to each other. No family can be happy where a right feeling is wanting on the part of brothers and sisters. Nothing can be a substitute for this defect, and it is of great importance that all young people should have this set in a proper light before them. Many households are a constant scene of confusion, a perpetual field of strife, and an affecting spectacle of misery, through the quarrels and ill will of those, who as flesh of each other's flesh, and blood of each other's blood, ought to have towards each other, no feeling but that of love, and to use no words but those of kindness.

I will divide the fraternal duties into three kinds: into those that are appropriate to the season of *childhood* —of *youth*—of *manhood*.

The general principles which are to regulate the discharge of these duties, and on which indeed they rest, are the same in reference to all seasons of life. Love, for instance, is equally necessary, whether brothers and sisters are sporting together in the nursery, dwelling together as young men and women beneath the parental roof, or descending the hill of life at the head of separate establishments and families of their own. Over and above the feelings of friendship, or of moral esteem, there must be those of complacency in them, as related to us by the ties of consanguinity; a consciousness, that by the dispensations of providence in uniting them to us by a bond of nature, and which nothing but death can dissolve, they have acquired a claim upon our efforts to make them happy, which is stronger than that of any strangers, except it be in those cases, where our brothers and sisters have by their unkind and cruel conduct, thrown off every thing but their name, and the stranger has assumed towards us the heart of a brother. And even in this case, we must still consider that they are our brothers, mourn their alienation with grief, view their aberrations with pity, watch them in their wanderings with an anxious interest, and keep the way open for their return to our fellowship. Children of the same parent who are wanting in love, are wanting in the first virtue of a brother and a sister as such. It is true, they may find companions more to their taste, considered as mere subjects of intellectual or general companionship, persons of more agreeable manners, of more pleasing tempers, of more cultivated minds ; but these are not brothers, nor must the perception, which in some cases it is impossible to avoid, of their great superiority in many respects, destroy that natural impulse, which the heart ought ever to feel and to obey, towards a brother or a sister. This love must of course be increased or diminished in its exercise, by circumstances, such as good or bad conduct, kindness or unkindness, but nothing must destroy the principle. The scripture, which is so replete with admonitions on almost every other subject, has said little on this : it has left nature spontaneously to send forth its fraternal energies ; and though containing many exhortations to the children of God to abound in brotherly love, has said little on this topic to the children of men ; a reserve which seems rather to imply that the duty is so obvious and so easy, as not to need an injunction, than that the discharge of it is not obligatory or not important. A child, a youth, or a man, who feels no goings forth of his heart, no peculiar interest, no appropriate and restrictive emotions towards a brother or a sister, is wanting in one of those social virtues, which it was certainly the intention of Providence should arise out of the relative ties.

But I will now go on to state how the various fraternal duties should be discharged in CHILDHOOD.

Brothers and sisters should make it a study to promote each other's happiness. They should take pleasure in pleasing each other, instead of each being selfishly taken up in promoting his own separate enjoyment. They should never envy each other's gratification; if one has a more valuable plaything than the other, the rest should rather rejoice than be sorry. Envy in children is likely to grow into a most baleful and malignant disposition. They should never take each other's possessions away, and be always willing to lend what cannot be divided, and to share what *does* admit of being divided. Each must do all he can to promote the happiness of the whole. They should never be indifferent to each other's sorrows, much less laugh at, and sport with each other's tears and griefs. It is a lovely sight to see one child weeping because another is in distress. A boy that sees his brother or sister weep, and can be unconcerned or merry at the sight, would when he becomes a man, in all probability, see them starve without helping them. Children should never accuse each other to their parents, nor like to see each other punished. An informer is a hateful and detestable character; but an informer against his brother or sister, is the most detestable of all spies. If, however, one should see another doing that which is wrong, and which is known to be contrary to the will of their parents, he should first in a kind and gentle manner point out the wrong, and give an intimation that if it be not discontinued, he shall be obliged to mention it:

and if the warning be not taken, it is then manifestly his duty to acquaint their parents with the fact. They must not tease or torment one another. How much domestic uneasiness sometimes arises from this source: one of the children, perhaps, has an infirmity or weakness of temper, or awkwardness of manner, or personal deformity, and the rest, instead of pitying it, tease and torment the unhappy individual, till all get quarrelling and crying together. Is this promoting their mutual comfort? If there be any one of the family that is in bad health, or weakly, all the rest, instead of neglecting that one, ought to strive to the uttermost to amuse him. How pleasing a sight it is, to see a child giving up his play time, to read to, or converse with, a sick brother or sister; while nothing is more disgusting than that selfishness which will not spare a single hour for the amusement of the poor sufferer upon the bed, or the little prisoner in the nursery. As to fighting, quarrelling, or calling ill names, this is so utterly disgraceful, that it is a deep shame upon those children who live in such practices. Dr. Watts has very beautifully said:—

> " Whatever brawls disturb the street,
>   There should be peace at home,
> Where sisters dwell, and brothers meet
>   Quarrels should never come.
>
> " Birds in their little nests agree;
>   And 'tis a shameful sight,
> When children of one family,
>   Fall out, and chide, and fight.

"Hard names at first, and threat'ning words,
That are but noisy breath,
May grow to clubs and naked swords,
To murder and to death."

Children that are removed from home to school, should be both watchful over, and kind to each other. They should manifest a peculiar and kind interest in each other's comfort, and not neglect one another. It is pleasant to see two brothers or two sisters, always anxious to have each other as playmates, or as members of the little circle with which they associate, defending one another from oppression or unkindness, and striving to make their absence from home, as comfortable as they can by their mutual kindness.

I go on now to shew in what way brothers and sisters should behave towards each other, during THE SEASON OF YOUTH.

I now suppose them to have arrived at the age of fourteen, and state their obligations between that period and the time when they settle in life. There should of course be a *tender attachment*, which becomes stronger and more visible, as they acquire a greater power of reason to understand their relationship and the design of Providence in forming this relation. Instead of this, however, we sometimes see brothers and sisters become more and more indifferent to each other, as they recede farther from the period of infancy. They should now reason upon the closeness of their relationship, and let the understanding give an additional impulse to their hearts. They should be *fond of each other's society,* and *put forth all their ingenuity to please one another.* It would have a delightful influence upon their mutual attachment, if their little separate proportion of pocket money were sometimes employed in making each other presents. How happy a state of feeling would be produced, if a sister, after having incidently expressed a wish for some little article, were to be surprised soon after by finding that a brother had, unknown to her, purchased the elegant or useful trifle, and placed it upon her toilet or work table. Sisters should put forth all their assiduity to provide for brothers whatever the needle can do for their personal accommodation, and feel a hallowed delight in giving their labour to increase the comforts and conveniences of those, whom it should be their study to please. A family of grown up children, should be the constant scene of uninterrupted harmony, where love, guided by ingenuity, puts forth all its power to please, by those mutual good offices, and minor acts of beneficence, of which every day furnishes the opportunity, and which, while they cost little in the way either of money or labour, contribute so much to the happiness of the household. One of the most delightful sights in our world, where there is so much moral deformity to disgust, and so much unkindness to distress, is a domestic circle, where the parents are surrounded by their children, of which, the daughters are being employed in elegant or useful work, and the elder brother reading some instructive and improving volume, for the benefit or entertainment of the whole. This is the scene which more than justifies the beautiful apostrophe of the sweetest and most tender of all poets :—

> "Domestic happiness, thou only bliss
> Of Paradise, that hast survived the fall!
> Though few now taste thee unimpaired and pure,
> Or, tasting, long enjoy thee; too infirm,
> Or too incautious to preserve thy sweets
> Unmixt with drops of bitter, which neglect
> Or temper sheds into thy chrystal cup.
> Thou art the nurse of virtue—in thine arms
> She dwells, appearing, as in truth, she is,
> Heav'n born, and destined to the skies again.
> Thou art not known, where pleasure is ador'd,
> That reeling goddess with the zoneless waist,
> And wand'ring eyes, still leaning on the arm
> Of novelty, her fickle, frail support:
> For thou art meek and constant, hating change,
> And finding, in the calm of truth tried love,
> Joys that her stormy raptures never yield.
> Forsaking thee, what shipwreck have we made
> Of honour, dignity, and fair renown!"

Scenes are to be found, but alas, how rarely, which give meaning and force to these lovely strains. Young people, seek your happiness in each other's society. What can the brother find in the circle of dissipation, or amongst the votaries of intemperance to compare with this? What can the sister find amidst the concert of sweet sounds, that has music for the soul compared with this domestic harmony? Or in the glitter and fashionable confusion, and mazy dance of the ball room, compared with these pure, calm, sequestered joys, which are to be found at the fire-side of a happy family? What can the theatre yield that is comparable with this?

> " 'Oh, ev'nings, worthy of the gods!' exclaim'd
> The Sabine bard. Oh, ev'nings, I reply,
> More to be priz'd, and coveted than yours,
> As more illumin'd, and with nobler truths,
> That I, and mine, and those we love, enjoy.
> Cards were superfluous here, with all the tricks
> That idleness has ever yet contriv'd
> To fill the void of an unfurnish'd brain;
> To palliate dullness, and give time a shove."

I would advise all young people to read "The Task," and especially the fourth book; and to read it, till they grow in love with those pure and hallowed home-born pleasures, which are at once the most atttainable and the most satisfying of any to be found in our curse-stricken world.

It is of great importance to the pleasant intercourse of brothers and sisters, that *each should pay particular attention to the cultivation of the temper.* I have known all the comfort of a family destroyed by the influence of one passionate or sullen disposition. Where such a disposition unhappily exists, the subject of it should take pains to improve it, and the other branches of the family, instead of teazing, or irritating, or provoking it, should exercise all possible forbearance, and with ingenious kindness help their unfortunate relative in the difficult business of self-control.

As woman seems formed by nature to execute the offices of a nurse, *sisters should be peculiarly kind and tender to sick brothers;* for there are few things which tend more to conciliate affection, than sympathy with us in our sufferings, and all those gentle and willing efforts, which, if they cannot mitigate our pains, have such a power to soothe our minds and divert our attention from the sense of suffering.

Mutual respect should be shown by brothers and sisters; all coarse, vulgar, degrading terms and modes of address should be avoided; and nothing but what is courteous, either done or said. The intercourse of such relatives should be marked, not indeed by the stiffness of ceremony, nor the coldness of formality, not the cautious timidity of suspicion, but by the politeness of good manners, blended with all the tenderness of love. It is peculiarly requisite also, that while this is maintained at home, there should not be disrespectful neglect in company. It is painful for a sister to find herself more neglected than the veriest stranger, and thus exposed to others as one in whom her brother feels no interest.

Brothers ought not, even in lesser matters, to be *tyrants over their sisters,* and expect from them the obsequiousness of slaves. The poor girls are sometimes sadly treated, and rendered miserable by the caprice, and freaks, and iron yoke of some insolent and lordly boy. Where the parents are living, they ought not to suffer such oppression. Of such a despot let all young women beware, for he that is a tyrant to his sister, is sure to be a tyrant also to a wife.

It is of great consequence, that brothers and sisters should maintain epistolary correspondence when absent from each other. It must be a very strong regard which separation, especially when it is for a long time, does not diminish. Flames burn brightest in the vicinity of each other. An affectionate letter received from an absent friend, tends to fan the dying spark of affection. They who can be long separated without such a bond as this, are already in a state of indifference to each other, and are in rapid progress to still wider alienation.

Brothers and sisters should be very careful, *not to become estranged from each other after the death of their parents;* of which there is always some danger. While one parent remains, though the other be gone to the sepulchre, there is a common centre of family affection still left, by drawing near to which, the members are kept near to each other; but when this survivor has also departed, the point of union is gone, and the household is likely, without great watchfulness to be divided and distracted. How often does this happen by the division of the family property?* The grave has scarcely closed over the parental remains, before strife, confusion, and every evil work begin in reference to the patrimonial possessions. To guard

* This, perhaps, rather belongs to the third division of the subject.

against this, the father should ever have his will made, a will made upon the obvious principles of wisdom and equity. Any attempt on the part of one child, to turn a parent's mind from the line of strict impartiality and equity towards the others ; any advantage taken of opportunities of more frequent access, to the parental ear and prejudices, to gain more than a just share of his property, is an act so base, so foul, and wicked, as to deserve the most severe, and impassioned, and indignant reprehension. Even in this case, however, the injured branches of the family, should not so far resent the matter, as to withdraw from all intercourse with the supplanter : remonstrate they may, and abate something of their esteem and regard they must, but still they are required by scripture to forgive him, and not to cherish hatred, or to manifest revenge. Unless in cases of unusual and extraordinary rapacity, the fraternal intercourse ought not to be stopped by unfair advantages of this kind.

There are instances, however, in which an *unequal* division of property, is not an *unjust* one, and ought not to be felt as such, by the party which receives the lesser share. If one child has become possessed of wealth from another source, I do not think that he ought to consider himself unfairly dealt with, if he do not receive so large a portion of the family property, as his brothers and sisters do. Or if there be one branch of the family, prevented, by the visitations of Providence from all active labour, the rest ought not to think it unfair, if a parent make a larger provision for this deformed or helpless child, than for the other branches. The alienation of brothers and sisters on account of pecuniary matters, is usually a matter of deep disgrace to them *all* ; not only to the spoiler, but also to the rest.

But in what terms shall I depict the atrocious wickedness of a villainous brother, who, after the death of their parents, would employ his influence to wheedle and swindle an unmarried sister out of her property, and reduce her to poverty and dependance, to indulge his own rapacity, or to avert calamity from himself? Such wretches *have* existed, and *do* exist; who, taking advantage of a sister's strong affection, combined with her ignorance of money matters, never cease, till, by all the arts of subtlety, they have got out of her possession the last shilling she has in the world; and then, perhaps, when she has nothing more for them to pilfer, abandon the victim of their cruelty, with the remorselessness of a highwayman, to want and misery. Let such monsters remember, that there is one in heaven whose eye has been upon all their wicked arts and cruel robbery, and who, for all these things will bring them into judgment. It is an act of cruelty in any brother, who, without any dishonest intention perhaps, would wish to jeopardise the property of a sister, in order either to increase his own gains, or to avert his own dreaded misfortunes. *She* may be very unfitted to struggle with poverty, and altogether disqualified for earning support by her own industry, and therefore ought not to be exposed to the danger of losing her property. Cases do occur sometimes, in which it may be proper, and even necessary, for the property of unmarried sisters to be employed in the trade of their brothers; but as a general rule, it is *unadvisable:* and where it does happen, the latter should let all their conduct be conducted on the principles of the greatest caution, the most rigid integrity, and the noblest generosity.

Brothers ought ever, after the death of their parents, to consider themselves as the natural guardians of unmarried sisters; their advisers in difficulty, their comforters in distress, their protectors in danger, their sincere, tender, liberal, and unchanging friends, amidst all the scenes and vicissitudes of life. It is rarely adviseable that a sister should permanently dwell with a married brother; but then, even the much stronger claims of the wife, ought not to cancel or throw into oblivion those of the sister.

I will now suppose the case of one or more branches of the family, who are brought by divine grace, to be partakers of true religion; and point out what is their duty to the rest, and what the duty of the rest to them. In reference to the former, it is manifestly their solemn and irrevocable obligation, to seek, by every affectionate, scriptural, and judicious effort, the real conversion of those of the family who are yet living without heartfelt religion. O how often has the leaven of piety, when by divine mercy and power it has been laid in the heart of one of the family, spread through nearly the whole household. How often has fraternal love, when it has soared to its sublimest height, and with a heaven kindled ambition aimed at the loftiest object which benevolence can possibly pursue, by seeking the salvation of a brother's soul, secured its prize, and received its rich reward. Young people, whose hearts are under the influence of piety, but whose hearts also bleed for those, who, though they are the children of the same earthly parent, are not yet the children of your Father in heaven, I call upon you by all the love you bear your brothers and sisters; by all the affection you bear for your parents ; by all the higher love you bear to God and Christ ; to seek by every proper means the conversion of those, who, though bound to you by the ties of nature, are not yet united by the bond of grace. Make it an object with you to win their souls. Pray for it constantly. Put forth in your own example all the beauties of holiness. Seek for the most undeviating consistency, since a single want of this would only strengthen the prejudice you are anxious to subdue. Let them *see* your religion in your conscientiousness, your joy, your humility, your meekness, your love. In all the general duties of life, be more than ordinarily exact. Win their affections by the kindest and most conciliating conduct. Avoid all consciousness of superiority. Attempt not to scold them out of their sins. Avoid the language of reproach. Draw them with the cords of love, for *they* are the bands of a man. Now and then recommend to their perusal a valuable book. When they are absent write to them on the subject of religion. But at the same time, do not disgust them by boring them with religion. Seize favourable opportunities, and wisely improve them. Point them to eminently happy, consistent, and useful chrsitians. Comply with all their wishes that are lawful, but give not up one atom of your consistency. Pliancy on your part to meet their tastes and pursuits, if they are contrary to God's word, will only disgust them ; mild firmness will secure their respect. And crown all with earnest prayer for that grace, without which no means can be successful. How knowest thou but thou shalt gain thy brother ? And O what a conquest !

And what shall be said to the *unconverted* party ? Shall such means be unsuccessful ? Will you resist this holy, benevolent influence ? Will you oppose these efforts to draw you to heaven ? Will you leave your sister to travel alone to the skies, and determine to separate from her for ever, and pursue your course to perdition ? Will you seek the dreadful, the fatal distinction, of being alone in your family as the enemy of God, the captive of Satan ? Shall a sister's solicitude for your salvation, and all the active efforts which it puts forth, be only a savour of death unto death to you ? Pause and ponder, young man ? Alter your purpose : take her by the hand, and say to her, " your affection has conquered, I will go with you, for I know that God is with you." But, perhaps, instead of this, you are a persecutor. What! a persecutor of religion, and of a sister, at the same time ? Yes, you reject with scorn these efforts for your salvation, and treat her with ridicule and unkindness by whom they are made. Is it so? What wicked enough for *this*? What carry your enmity to piety so far as to embitter the life of a sister, for no other reason than because she bows her heart to its influence? Recollect, the contest is not between you and her, but between you and God. It is not as a sister, but as a christian, that she is the object of your displeasure, and therefore your ill will is against religion, and if against religion, then against God, for religion is the image of God in the soul of his rational creatures. Did you ever read or hear that fearful denunciation? if not, read it now, —" Woe to him that contendeth with his maker." This woe is uttered against every persecutor of religion, and therefore is against you.

The responsibility of *elder* brothers and sisters, especially that of the FIRST BORN, is great indeed. They are looked up to by the younger branches of the family as examples, and their example has great influence, in some cases greater than that of the parent : it is the example of one more upon a level with themselves, more near to them, more constantly before them, than that of the parent, and is on these accounts more influential. It is of immense consequence, therefore, to their juniors, how these conduct themselves. If they are bad, they are likely to lead all the rest astray : if good, they may have great power in leading them aright. They bring companions, books, recreations, before the rest, which are proper or improper according as their own taste is. It is a most distressing spectacle to see an elder brother or sister training up younger ones, by his own conduct and precept, in the ways of wickedness. Such a youth is an awful character: like Satan he goeth about seeking whom by his temptations he may destroy; but worse, in some respects, more wicked and more cruel than his prototype, he marks out his own brother as the victim of his cruelty, and the dupe of his wiles. Whole families, have in some cases, been schooled in iniquity by one unprincipled elder son. What will such a brother have to answer for in the day of judgment, and what will be his torment in hell, when the souls of those whom he has ruined shall be near him, and by their ceaseless reproaches become his eternal tormentors. In other cases, what a blessing to a family has been a steady, virtuous, and pious elder brother or sister! Many a weak and sickly mother has given daily thanks to God for a daughter, who by her attentions was a kind of second mother to the younger members of the family, for whom she did her uttermost to train them up in her own useful and holy habits. Many a a father has felt with equal gratitude the blessing of having in his first born son, not only a help to himself in the cares of business, but in the work of education; a son who lent all the power of an amiable and religious example, to form the characters of his younger brothers. Let such young persons consider their responsibility, and at the same time let those who are their juniors in the family consider *their* duty. If they have a good example in their elder brothers and sisters, they should make it not only the object of attention and admiration, but also of imitation; but on the other hand, if, unhappily, the conduct of their seniors be bad, let them not follow them in their evil course; let no threats, no bribes, no persuasions, induce them to comply with the temptation to do what is wrong.

I have now to allude to the discharge of fraternal duties *during the whole period of our lives, after the season of youth has passed away.* This has been anticipated in part already. Families are soon broken up: the parents die, the children marry and form separate establishments, and bring around them separate families of their own. This division of the original stock does not however destroy, although it necessarily must weaken the fraternal tie. Pope beautifully remarks,

> " Thus beast and bird their common charge attend,
> The mothers nurse it, and the sires defend;
> The young dismissed to wander earth or air,
> There stops the instinct, and there ends the care:
> The link dissolves, each seeks a fresh embrace,
> Another love succeeds, another race.
> A longer care Man's helpless kind demands;
> That longer care contracts more lasting bands.
> Still as one brood, and as another rose,
> These *natural* love maintained, *habitual* those.
> Reflection, reason, still the ties improve,
> At once extend the interest and the love;
> And still new needs, new helps, new habits rise;
> That graft benevolence on charities."

Great care is necessary, however, that when the

centre of fraternal charities is gone, and each child becomes himself a centre of similar emotions and impulses, the interest of brothers and sisters in each other, does not altogether cease. Brothers and sisters are brothers and sisters still, though they dwell in different quarters of the globe, are each at the head of families of their own, are distinguished in their circumstances by the varieties of affluence and poverty, and have attained to the age of threescore years and ten : and the tie that unites them ought to be *felt* coiling round their hearts, and its influence ought to be seen in producing all those tender offices, which a common relationship to the same parent, certainly demands. The next generation may, from various causes, lose their interest in each other. Regard for remote relations, becomes in every country, less and less, according as law extends its protection, commerce diffuses its wealth, and civilization multiplies its comforts. Where clanship is necessary for mutual protection, " the families that spring from one common stock, continue to cling to each other for aid, almost as if they lived together under the same roof: it is truly one wide family, rather than a number of families; the history of the tribe in its remote years of warfare and victory, is the history of each individual of the tribe; and the mere remembrance of the exploits of those who fought with one common object, around the representative of their common ancestor, is like the feeling of the fraternal or filial relation, prolonged from age to age. This is not the case, however, in that state of society in which *we* are placed, where the feeling of affectionate interest, of fraternal love, rarely survives the next generation from the father, and often dies long before *that* has completed its course. Brothers and sisters ought, however, to keep up, as long as they live, their mutual love. They should not suffer new, and it is confessed, still nearer relations, to produce a total oblivion of, or alienation from, each other. If dwelling in distant parts of the kingdom, epistolary correspondence should be maintained, sympathy in their mutual joys and sorrows should be cherished, occasional visits, as opportunity might allow, should be paid, and every thing done by mutual kind offices, to comfort each other, on the rough and stormy journey of life. If dwelling together in the same town, their intercourse should be such as to constrain spectators to exclaim, " Behold how good and pleasant it is for brethren to dwell together in unity." There should be that tenderness, which would lead to all the delicate attentions that affection delights to pay, and at the same time that confidence, which would prevent offence from being taken, when these were hindered by accident from being paid. How utterly disgraceful is it to see brothers and sisters dwelling together in the same town, yet living in a state of continual strife, and sometimes in an utter suspension of all intercourse. In such cases there must be faults on both sides, though not perhaps, in equal proportions. Those who marry into a family should be very cautious not to carry discord into it. Not unfrequently has it happened, that brothers have been embroiled by their wives, and sisters by their husbands; and they who till they were married, scarcely ever had an angry word from each other, scarcely ever lived in peace afterwards. Happy and honourable is that family, which, though it consists of numerous branches, and those, perhaps, nearly all married, and dwelling in the same vicinity, maintains, not indeed a state of coldness and formal intercourse, of which the highest praise is that it is free from strife, but a fellowship of sympathy, helpfulness and love.

If by the vicissitudes of life, and the various allotments of divine Providence, one branch of the family has been more successful than the rest, peculiar care must be exercised, that the latter should not expect too much from him in the way of attention and relief, nor the former yield too little. For any man to be ashamed of his poor brothers and sisters, to treat them with cold neglect or insulting pride, discovers a littleness of mind which deserves contempt, and a depravity of heart which merits our severest indignation: it is at once ingratitude to God and cruelty to man. It must be admitted, however, that it is extremely difficult to meet the demands, and satisfy the expectations of poor relations, especially in those cases where their poverty is the fruit of their own indolence or extravagance. They have claims, it is acknowledged, and a good brother or sister will readily allow, and cheerfully meet them; but it must be for prudence, under the guidance of affection, to adjust their amount. It is unquestionable, however, that though there are some few, who have most indiscreetly impoverished themselves, to help a needy, perhaps an undeserving brother or sister, the multitude have erred on the other side. Men or women of wealth, who choose to live in celibacy, and who have needy brothers and sisters, are cruel and hard hearted creatures, if they suffer such relatives to want any thing for their real comfort. " Whoso hath this world's good, and seeth his brother have need, and shutteth up his bowels of compassion from him, how dwelleth the love of God in him." And what shall be said of those, who, in bequeathing their property, forget their poor relations? The man who passes over a poor brother or sister and their families, to endow a hospital, or enrich the funds of a religious society, to which, perhaps, he gave next to nothing while he lived, offers robbery for a burnt offering.

I have now said all that appears to me to be important on the subject of fraternal duties. Is it necessary to call in the aid of motives to enforce the discharge of *such* obligations? If so,

Let *your parents' comfort* be a plea with you. How often have the hearts of such been half broken by the feuds of their children? And even where the calamity has not gone to this extent, their cup has been embittered by the wranglings, quarrels, and perpetual strifes of those who ought to have lived in undisturbed affection.

Your own comfort and honour are involved in an attention to these duties. You cannot neglect the claims of a brother or a sister, without suffering a diminution in your happiness, or your reputation, or both.

The interests of society demand of you an attention to fraternal claims. As a son, you learn to be a good subject, as a brother, you learn to be a good citizen. Rebellious children are traitors in the bud: and he who has none of the right feelings of a brother, is training up for a parricide.

And as to *religion*—fraternal duties necessarily arise out of its general principles, are enforced by its prevailing spirit more than by particular precepts, and are recommended by some of its most striking examples, for the first murder which stained the earth with human gore, sprung from a want of brotherly affection; and the family in which the Son of God found his loved retreat on earth, was that, where in the persons of Mary, and Martha, and Lazarus, fraternal love was embodied and adorned.

CHAPTER VIII.

THE DUTIES OF MASTERS.

"Ye masters, do the same things unto them, forbearing threatening; knowing that your master also is in heaven; neither is there respect of persons with him."

EPHES. vi. 9.

"Masters give unto your servants, that which is just and equal."

COL. iv. 1.

"A party of friends setting out together upon a journey, soon find it to be best for all sides, that while they are upon the road, one of the company should wait upon the rest; another ride forward to seek out lodging and entertainment; a third to carry the portmanteau; a fourth take charge of the horses; a fifth bear the purse, conduct and direct the route; not forgetting, however, that as they were equal and independent when they set out, so they are all to return to a level at their journey's end. The same regard and respect; the same forbearance, lenity, and reserve, in using their service; the same mildness in delivering commands; the same study to make their journey comfortable and pleasant, which he whose lot it was to direct the rest, would in common decency think himself bound to observe towards them, ought we to shew towards those, who, in the casting of the parts of human society, happen to be placed within our power, or to depend upon us."

PALEY.

"There are duties which we owe to the lowest of those who serve us, that are not fulfilled by the most bountiful allotment of wages, and lodging, and sustenance. Of these duties, which are not duties of supererogation, but flow from the very nature of the bond which connects the master and the servant by reciprocal benefits, the surest rule is to be found in that brief direction which Seneca, in the spirit of the noble christian precept of morals, has so happily given us in one of his epistles, in which he treats of the cruelty and contumely of Roman masters.—' So live with your inferior, as you would wish with your superior to live with you.' "

DR. THOMAS BROWN.

"It has been justly remarked, that all authority over others, is in fact, a talent with which we are entrusted for their benefit, as well as our own; and so the discharge of our duty to them is only, in other words, securing our own interest as well as theirs. This, however, is especially manifest in the case of servants dwelling under our roof as members of the same family. Thereby how much our care over the souls of our servants contributes to their knowledge of God and themselves, so far have we secured their conscientious regard to our interests and furnished them with principles, which will not only augment the stock of domestic happiness, but certainly contribute towards the divine favour resting on our dwelling, as well as on all we possess. Thus, then, is the fear of God in master and servant, found to be at once the only foundation of relative duty, and the only effectual security for the discharge of it."

ANDERSON.

"The highest panegyric that private virtue can receive, is the praise of servants, for they see a man without any restraint or rule of conduct, but such as he voluntarily prescribes to himself. And however vanity or ignorance may look down with contempt on the suffrage of men undignified by wealth, and unenlightened by education, it very seldom happens that they commend or blame without justice.

"The danger of betraying our weakness to our servants, and the impossibility of concealing it from them, may be justly considered as one motive to a regular and irreproachable life. For no condition is more hurtful and despicable, than his, who has put himself in the power of his servant; in the power of him, whom, perhaps, he has first corrupted, by making him subservient to his vices, and whose fidelity he therefore cannot enforce by any precepts of honesty or reason. From that fatal hour, when he sacrificed his dignity to his passions, he is in perpetual dread of insolence or defamation; of a controller at home, or an accuser abroad."

JOHNSON.

Of all the domestic connexions, that between master and servant, is perhaps least understood, or at any rate, most neglected. In the two preceding cases, nature, imperfect and corrupt as she is, has come in with her aid; but this is a connexion, affecting very extensively the vital interest of the family, but which is left by God to conscience and scripture alone. Should these two be neglected, what wonder if the duty on either side is not fulfilled. It is not a connexion founded on mutual love, like that of man and wife; nor in consanguinity, like that of parent and child, or brother and sister; but in mere convenience. It seems at first sight, a destruction of the natural equality of the human race, and an invasion by one party, of the rights of the other. It did not exist originally, but soon grew out of the natural course of things, such as the varied degrees of men's acquired property; the love of ease on the one hand, and the urgency of necessity on the other. It was wealth or power that made the first master; and want or weakness that made the first servant; and the very same circumstances which originated the relation preserves it. No one is servant by choice, but of necessity, and becomes a master as soon as he can. All this shews that there is great propriety and importance in stating with clearness, and enjoining with frequency, the duties of this connexion; and that there needs great impartiality in adjusting the claims of both parties so as to prevent the master from becoming a tyrant, and the servant from becoming a rebel; in other words to guard the master against the disobedience and dishonesty of the servant, and the servant against the oppression and cruelty of the master.

To the right performance of the Duties of Masters and Mistresses, the following qualifications are necessary.

1. A correct view of the nature and design of the family compact, as intended to train up all the members that compose it, to be good members of the civil community, and of the church of Christ. They must keep in constant recollection, that the domestic constitution has a reference to religion, to heaven, and to eternity; and that they who are appointed to be the head of it, are accountable to God for the manner in which they give it this direction. Every household is intended to be a seminary for virtue and piety, of which the master and mistress are the teachers; the servants as well as the children are the pupils.

2. They should be partakers of true religion.

Hence you see they are directed to consider, that they have a master in heaven, and to perform their duties with a believing and constant reference to their accountability to Christ. Without personal religion, they cannot of course seek on behalf of their servants the highest end of the domestic constitution, i. e. their spiritual and eternal welfare. Nor can they, without religion, be so well prepared to discharge even the ordinary duties of their station. True religion will not fail, wherever it exists in full vigour and operation, to teach a man, in reference *to every thing*, the best rules and ends, and measures of action; and especially will the grace of God, in this case, prevent that pride, passion, cruelty and unkindness, which make a man a bad master; and at the same time it will implant those virtues which are the germs of a master's greatest excellence. Religion is the strongest basis and the firmest support of authority; it not only renders all the commandments which are delivered, holy, and just, and good; not only infuses wisdom and equity into all the laws which are enjoined, but invests the lawgiver himself with the beauty of goodness, and the awful power of sanctity. A peculiar awe and dread seem to have been upon the inferior creatures, for man in his innocence, as a kind of reverence for the divine image which he bore; and the more holiness there is in a man's character now, the more power is there in his authority, and the more nearly does he come back to his original dominion, at least over the rational creation. If we would govern well, and easily, and pleasantly, we must inspire reverence rather than fear, and nothing does this like religion. " Them that honour me saith God, I will honour :" this is never more remarkably exemplified, than in the case of eminently holy masters and mistresses.

3. They should entertain correct notions of the nature and design of the relation they stand in to their servants, who are to be considered as their equals in nature, though their inferiors in rank; and not as beings of another and inferior race.

Servants are not mere speaking brutes, but rational men and women, who are bone of your bone, and flesh of your flesh, and who on the ground of natural equality, covenant with you to deliver to you so much service, for so much wages. They are your equals in the eye of the laws of the land, and are as much protected as you are; equal in the eye of God who is no respecter of persons; equal in personal formation, having the same corporeal senses, members and beauty, and the same mental faculties; equal in the church of God, being redeemed by the same blood of atonement, regenerated by the same holy spirit, and entitled to the same heaven; and on all these grounds justly claiming the respect that is due to a man and a christian; as such they are to be addressed and treated; and not spoken to and addressed like beasts.

I now lay down one or two preliminary remarks.

1. Professing christians should be very careful in the selection of their servants.

It is desirable, where it can be done, to engage such servants as are truly and consistently pious. I know that this cannot always be accomplished in reference to the household, much less in the manufactory and the shop. In a business that depends upon the skill of the workmen, a master must have such as will suit his purpose, whether they possess moral qualifications or not. But when he cannot get good men he should endeavour to reform, to the extent of his ability, such as are bad. It must be admitted that there are many, both men and women, who, as to their general qualifications are most excellent servants, who yet do not possess true piety; they are industrious, good tempered, honest and cleanly, and contribute far more to the comfort of the families that employ them, than some conceited, cross, and indolent professors of religion. Notwithstanding this, it is every way desirable to obtain, if we can, those to serve us, who, we have every reason to believe, serve the Lord Christ.

Other things being equal, pious servants are much to be preferred to those who are without the fear of God. They may bring the blessing of God with them into your house. You have the benefit of their example and of their prayers: in the time of sickness, you have the consolation of their remarks as well as their sympathy: and hence they have been, in many cases, sources of inconceivable comfort to the households, in which they have been placed. If you have a family, how immensely important is this matter. Think of what incalculable mischief one unprincipled servant may be the author, in a circle of young children. On this account, if a person of decided piety cannot be found, at least determine that none but such as are strictly moral, shall be inmates in your habitation. David determined that no liar should dwell in his family. The utmost caution should be exercised, to keep from the *nursery* all improper persons. Nor ought any mother to trust her children too much to any servants, however excellent; and on admitting them, she should very minutely instruct them in all those points of conduct towards the minds of their children, as well as their bodies, both what they are to avoid, and what they are to observe. " I would sooner take a toad into my bosom," said an old author, " than a wicked servant into my family." Well might he say this, for the poor reptile is belied in being said to be armed with poison, but the wicked servant has poison for the mind both of her fellow servants and the children. Christian parents are not perhaps sufficiently cautious on this head. They are not sufficiently impressed with the importance of the subject, till they learn it by the various kinds of mischief that have been done. The present age has peculiar advantages for a good selection, inasmuch as by the extension of education, many young women of considerable respectability, are trained for the important situation of nursery governesses.

2. When you engage a servant, let there be a very explicit statement of what each party expects from the other.

The master or mistress should most fully explain to the servant, all that will be demanded in the way of service, and all that will be given in the way of wages, and of privileges, both temporal and spiritual. Nothing should be concealed, or omitted to be brought forward at some future time; this is in the highest degree dishonourable, and subjects the encroaching party to the justest reproach. It would be well for you to inform your servants, in a very minute and particular manner, of all the religious habits of your family, and what compliance with these you will expect from them.

The duties of Masters and Mistresses may be classed under three heads.

First. You owe them a duty of JUSTICE.

This demands, *that you should give them a fair remuneration for their labour.* The amount should not only be enough to support them in mere existence, but in comfort. It is an utter disgrace to any man, much more to a professing christian, to abate and screw down those whom he employs, till they cannot earn enough for their decent clothing, and the nourishment of their strength. Is not this to grind the faces of the poor? But, as in *trade,* there are certain rates of wages, from which it may be difficult for a master, however pious or humane, to vary, I shall merely remark, that such men ought never to be forward in lowering the price of labour, beyond what is actually necessary to keep possession of the market. As to *household* servants, to whom this chapter more especially applies, it is very dishonourable to a mistress to higgle about a few shillings, with a poor dependant creature, whom she is scarcely willing should earn enough to procure herself reputable apparel. I do not wish servants to be encouraged in dress, and in expensive habits: there is too great a propensity to this in many young women, which ought to be checked, and if it can be done by no other means, by a reduction of wages. But enough ought to be afforded in all cases, for suitable attire, and for a little surplus fund, which they should be encouraged to make against a time of destitution and helplessness. If we do not furnish them by a sufficiency of wages, with the means of honestly supplying their wants, are we not tempting them to make up the deficiency by dishonesty? And of course, their wages should be regularly paid. It is disreputable to be long in debt to any one, but utterly scandalous, when such creditors are unpaid servants, who ask, without success, for what has been due to them for months. I wonder the pride, if not the principle of some people, does not prevent them from putting on new finery, while the servants in the kitchen are saying, "That bonnet and gown are mine, for I am owed the money which paid for them, if indeed they *be* paid for."

Justice demands that you should pay your servants for *all the work they do;* and that every thing, which in respect of time or labour, is above the stipulated or usual quantity of service rendered for a given sum, should be most equitably paid for. There are some persons who are proverbially mean, for exacting, not only what is actually due to them for the wages they pay, but for getting, if possible, a little extra service without paying for it: this remark applies, of course, to the case of day work. If a woman be hired to work in the parlour, or the kitchen, or a man be engaged for the garden, such persons will generally detain them if they can, an hour or two beyond the usual time, on pretence, perhaps, of finishing up the matter, or getting ready something of importance. This would be all very fair, if they paid an extra sum for the extra work; but, no! they want the additional hour or two to be thrown in for nothing. But when the case is reversed, and the workman or woman is obliged to go away an hour or two earlier than the usual time, they are then forward enough to make a deduction from the amount paid to them. This is not only detestably mean, but actually dishonest, for it is taking the labouring person's work without paying for it. Many persons, and some of them professors of religion, have no conscience in this matter, and get a character for extortionate selfishness from all whom they employ. In our money transactions with those who serve us, we should always lean to the side of generosity, or at least, should pay to the uttermost farthing, for all the work which is done for us.

Justice requires, *that your domestic servants be well provided for in all the necessaries and accommodations of life.* Their food should be wholesome and sufficient; their lodging should be such as is convenient for them in respect to warmth and protection, and not such as a person of even tolerable humanity would scarcely allot to the dogs of his flock. If people cannot really afford to give such wages as will procure decent attire, nor such food, both as to quantity and quality, as is necessary to keep up the strength of a servant, they ought not to have one, and should do the work themselves. I pity from the very bottom of my heart some poor orphans, hired perhaps, if not from the workhouse, yet from friends that are glad to get them off their hands at any price, who although burdened with excessive labour, are not allowed meat and drink sufficient to support their strength, and to nourish their stunted frame, and are in a condition, which, with the single exception of liberty, is more pitiable than that of many African slaves. Medicine and surgical assistance, also, should be procured for our domestic servants at our cost, as long as they are in our employ. I do not like the practice of hurrying them off, except in the case of contagious diseases, to hospitals and dispensaries, and thus calling upon the public to provide for the relief of those, whose cases belong to us. Much less is it equitable to make them pay the expences of their own affliction. We have known servants who were half beggared by doctors' bills, which ought to have been discharged by those in whose service they contracted the ailments which reduced them to suffering and poverty.

Justice also equally demands, *in the case of apprentices, that they should be well taught the business which they come to you to learn; especially, where, as in many cases, a high premium is paid for this very purpose.* No man can honestly retain such property, or indeed, such apprentice with whom it is given, if he do not even take pains to instruct him. If there be any secret in the trade, it must be thrown open to him, for he comes to you for that very purpose. Nor is it enough not to hinder him from acquiring the business, but you must take pains to help him. I do think that this circumstance is very much forgotten by masters, not excepting those that make a profession of religion. Apprentices, I know, are taken with a primary view to the master's interest: but in return for the help which a servant affords towards the accomplishment of this object, a master covenants to instruct him in the trade, and the man who employs an apprentice in any thing else than that which he came to learn, and suffers him through his neglect, to remain ignorant of the trade, is guilty of a double act of robbery: he robs the parent of the youth of his property, and at the same time, robs the youth himself of all his future means and opportunities of success.

Justice demands, *that when they leave your service, you should dismiss them, as far as you are able, consistently with truth, with a good character.* Their character is their wealth, and if this be gone, their means of subsistence have all vanished. Do not disallow them the right of leaving you when they please, nor avenge yourselves upon them by insinuating any thing to their disadvantage. On the contrary, do all you can to raise their reputation, and say all the good you can in their favour.

" There is a carelessness and facility, in ' giving

characters,' as it is called," says Paley, "especially, when given in writing, or according to some established form, which, to speak plainly of it, is a cheat upon those who accept them. They are given with so little reserve and veracity, ' that I should as soon depend, says the author of the Rambler, upon an acquittal at the Old Bailey by way of recommendation of a servant's honesty, as upon one of these ' characters.' It is sometimes carelessness: and sometimes to get rid of a bad servant, without the uneasiness of a dispute; for which nothing can be pleaded but the most ungenerous of all excuses, that the person whom we deceive is a stranger.

" There is a conduct the reverse of this, but more injurious, because the injury falls where there is no remedy; I mean the obstructing of a servant's advancement, because you are unwilling to spare his service. To stand in the way of your servant's interest, is a poor return for his fidelity, and affords slender encouragement for good behaviour, in this numerous, and therefore important part of the community. It is a piece of injustice, which if practised towards an equal, the law of honour would lay hold of; as it is, it is neither uncommon nor disreputable."

It is but common justice also, *to do something for the provision of servants that have worn themselves out in your service.* To leave such to penury and want in the wintry season of their old age, is an instance of great and disgraceful cruelty. How much have they contributed either to your wealth or to your comfort, and perhaps to both. By the Levitical law it was provided, that a servant who had been six years in the employ of a master, should be treated with great generosity. "He shall not," said the Lord, "be sent empty away; but thou shalt furnish him liberally out of thy flock, out of thy floor, and out of thy wine press; and that wherewith the Lord thy God hath blessed thee, thou shalt give unto him."—(Deut. xv. 13, 14.) Now if six year's service, under the law, were considered to entitle a servant to such an acknowledgment, surely a whole life's labour under the gospel dispensation, entitles them in their old age to no less. I ask this, not on the ground of kindness, but of justice; for it partakes of oppression and extortion, to give them no more for their time and strength than they need for the passing moment, and then to cast them upon the parish, when we can no longer render them subservient to our interests.

Secondly. KINDNESS comprehends another extensive class of duties owed by masters and mistresses to their servants.

You must be careful not to over work them.

A merciful man will not overload his beast. We have been often shocked to see in our streets, or on the public road, how cruelly some weak, half starved animals have been used, in being compelled to drag along burthens much beyond their strength: but are there not scenes of equal cruelty, to be witnessed in some houses, where is to be found a poor, young, friendless girl, whose pallid looks and delicate frame indicate to every one, but her hard hearted mistress, that she is incompetent to the tasks, which without cessation, she is mercilessly compelled to sustain? Her toil commences, perhaps, at five or six o'clock in the morning, and continues without intermission till eleven at night. Of work, she has too much for the robust and well nourished frame, especially for her weak and ill fed constitution. Some unfeeling creatures seem to think, that the payment of five or six pounds a year, gives them a right to exhaust all the energies of the poor hapless beings who are unfortunate enough to be employed by them. And even where unkindness is not carried to this extent, I am persuaded that servants are in very many cases, quite overworked; they are so urged by incessant demands for their labour, that from the beginning to the end of the week, they have scarcely a moment to keep their own clothing in proper repair, much less to attend to the concerns of their souls: their employers seem to think, that every moment they sit down, is so much time stolen from them. Are there any *professing christians* who act thus? Yes: and in so far they are a disgrace to the christian name.

Your method of addressing them, while it accords with your station, and partakes of the dignity of superiority, should be as remote from bitterness and contemptuous pride, as it is from familiarity. Do not speak to them as if they were a race of inferior creatures, whom it almost demeaned you to notice. There are some masters and mistresses, who though they do not swear, or storm, or call reproachful names, yet have a method of addressing their servants, which they would scarcely use to a brute animal. I have myself heard tones, and seen looks, which the authors of them would not, and did not give to their dogs. Servants are not stocks and stones, but men and women; and how galling to their feelings, how insulting to their rank as rational creatures, must it be to be addressed as a reptile race, who were scarcely entitled to the most common civilities. And as *pride* is improper, so is *passion*. Masters are commanded to "forbear threatening." This is particularly specified, because there is a great proneness to this in many, if not in most persons. When an inferior displeases us, the temptation to undue sallies of wrath, gusts of passion, and threatening words, is peculiarly strong. The individual is so much below us, and in our power, that let us say what we will, we have nothing to fear in return. But how mean and cowardly, and execrable is it, to say nothing of the wickedness of such conduct, for any one to hector, and bully, and threaten a poor, defenceless creature, because he has no need to apprehend any thing in the way of revenge. We must as christians, not only be meek, and gentle, and patient, but be gentle towards all, to those who are *below* us, as well as to those who are above us. Occasions will, of course, often present themselves, when it will be necessary to find fault, and to *express* displeasure: but this should never be done in a passion. A fury never can be respectable: we never go into a rage without disgracing ourselves in the eyes of our servants: at such times we may be terrible, but we cannot be reputable. Abusive epithets and ill names lower our dignity, and undermine our authority. Mild firmness, rational expostulation, and meek reproof, will do far more, both in the way of punishing faults, and of reforming them, than petulance and passion. Speak kindly to them, then, at all times. Let your words, and even your tones, partake of a dignified courtesy, blending and softening authority with good will. At the same time, *avoid all familiarity*, and do not encourage an obtrusive and encroaching boldness. You must keep *them* in their place, and in order to this, you must keep *yours*. Do nothing to remove the line of demarcation between you, nor encourage them to step over it. You must not joke with them, nor make yourselves merry with them; you must not enter into gossip with them about the floating occurrences of the neighbourhood, nor encourage them to bring you tales, nor employ them as your purveyors of scandal. Some persons, who would not run the risk of being thought busy bodies themselves, scruple not to encourage their servants to bring them all the news of the town. All this is mischievous in the highest degree, and tends to degrade those who are foolish enough to indulge in it, in the eyes of those who should be taught to respect them.

You should manifest an unvarying regard for their comfort. Take a deep interest in their welfare, and make it clear to them that you wish to see them happy.

Watch over their health, tenderly inquire into the cause of their ailments, and by mitigating their labour, and procuring them medical assistance, do all you can for their recovery. Advise them for their good, and refuse not your counsel whenever it can be of service to them. Convince them by the whole of your conduct, that you are their real friends, and truly anxious to make them happy and respectable.

Bear with patience those lesser infirmities which may comport with substantial excellences. Do not be strict to mark, at least with severity, their more trivial faults. Some mistresses render their servants miserable by incessant complaint: they are such slaves to excessive neatness, that they are always in bondage themselves, and make every body miserable around them.

Kindness to servants, would lead us *to administer commendation as often as possible, and to censure with as much lenity, as a due regard to justice will allow.*

"There is a certain moral pleasure which we particularly owe them. They may do well, and in doing well, they have the same title to our praise, which our best actions have to the glory with which we expect the world to be ready to reward us. If we withhold the approbation which is due, we take from them one powerful incentive to continuance of that species of conduct which rendered them worthy of approbation; and at the same time, we take from them one of the most delightful feelings of which he who has sold his freedom is still capable—the feeling, that he has done something, which was not actually sold with the very labour of his hands—that in the additional duties performed by him, he has been free still, and that our praise is something, which, as it was not an actual condition, like the livery and the daily bread, is an offering to his own gratuitous virtue. The duty of approbation, then, when approbation is due, is another of the duties which the master owes to the servant; and a duty which, though he may legally withhold it, he is not entitled morally to withhold.

" But servants share not our love of praise only, but passions of a less commendable kind. They are assailed by temptations, like those which assail us, and they sometimes fall, as we too fall. They neglect to do what we have desired; and they often do what is positively injurious to us. In such cases, they might deserve all our severity of punishment, if we were not men, and they were not men. Our reproof they unquestionably deserve, not merely because they have failed in their part of our mutual contract, but also, because our reproof may, even to them be attended with moral advantage. Yet though our reproof of any gross inattention is not excusable only, but, if we consider all its consequences, an act of humanity, it is not to be the reproof of one who seems almost pleased with the offence itself, in the eagerness which is shown to reprehend it. In censuring, we are silently to have in mind the human weaknesses of our own moral nature; and to remember, that if even we, with better light, and nobler recreations, err, the ignorant, who by their very ignorance, are incapable of seeing many of the consequences of actions, and who have few recreations, but those which seduce them from what is good, may still more naturally be imagined to err. In condemning them, therefore, we condemn ourselves; or we declare that we are frail creatures, of whom less knowledge and less virtue are to be expected than from them. There are beings with gentle voices, and still gentler eyes, and with smiles that seem never to be willed, and scarcely even to fade and brighten again, but to be almost the native character of the countenance, like the very lustre that is ever blooming on the lip and on the cheek;—there are beings who seem to exist thus only in a perpetual moral atmosphere of radiance and serenity, that on the sight of a single particle of dust on a book, or a table, or a chair, as if in that particle a whole mountain of misery were before them, can assume in an instant, all the frowns and thunders of all the furies; whose delicate frame is too weak to bear the violent opening of a door, but not too weak, after the door is opened, to shake the very floor with the violence of their own wrath on the unfortunate opener of it."*

Kindness should lead us *to allow our servants all possible indulgences and recreations that are not incompatible with religion.*

They are capable of gratification like ourselves, and have the same desire of it; while at the same time, are denied by their very circumstances, access to

* Dr. Brown's Lectures.

many of those sources of delight which are continually open to us. Those who seem to grudge domestic servants an occasional remission of their labour, that they may have communion with others at the feast of innocent enjoyment, convert their service into slavery, and render the oppression additionally bitter by the circumstance, that it is exercised in the land of freemen. I have often been delighted to see the cheerful faces of female servants at those meetings which are convened for promoting the various objects connected with the cause of religion and humanity, and who seemed to drink in the streams of eloquence and piety, with as eager a thirst, and as exquisite an enjoyment, as their more enlightened and better educated masters and mistresses. And I have known those, who, when going to some neighbouring town or village to attend, perhaps, a religious service of a public nature, have placed a female servant on the box seat of the carriage that conveyed them, that she might share the pleasures of the day. It is our duty, of course, to keep them from all polluting and vitiating amusements, but it is not less a duty of benevolence, to give them as often as is convenient to us, and consistent with their interests, an opportunity of enjoying the liberty and the sunshine of innocent and holy pleasure.

It is no credit, but very much otherwise, to any family, to be always changing their servants. Some persons have as many as there are months in the year. Their place has acquired so bad a reputation, that no good servant will offer herself for it. It is astonishing how extensively the character of every household is known amongst persons of this description. Those who keep register offices, can tell, perhaps, the repute in which most of the families in a town are held, for oftentimes upon mentioning a house to one who has applied for a place of service, they receive some such reply as this :—" I will not offer myself there, for I shall not be kept above a month or two if I go." This is not to the honour of any one, much less to the professor of religion : for, as those who leave the place, are naturally enough anxious to justify themselves to their friends, they scruple not to tell all the faults of their mistress, and oftentimes, of course, with great exaggeration, and thus the credit of religion suffers. Besides, what a risk is it, where there are children, to be always receiving fresh servants into the family : and what an interruption also to domestic comfort. Avoid then, unnecessary changes, and every thing that leads to them, whether it be bad temper, inflicting excessive labour, or striving after unattainable perfection.

A kind master or mistress *will prevent their servants from being* INSULTED OR OPPRESSED BY THE CHILDREN. It is really affecting to see what cruel scorn and impertinence, are, in some families, allowed to be practised towards respectable men and women, by those little tyrant masters and misses, whose weak parents never allow them to be opposed in any thing. They may utter the grossest falsehoods, indulge in the most wanton and distressing vexation, vent the most scurrilous abuse, and utter the foulest epithets against the servants, and their pitiless and unjust mother or father, with the full knowledge of the fact, allow this cruel insolence to continue. Children ought not to be permitted in any kind or degree to be guilty of such impropriety as this. They should be kept from being familiar, but equally so from being impertinent. I would never allow a servant to strike children, nor to be struck, or in any way oppressed *by* them.

Peculiar attention, partaking at once of respect and kindness should be shewn to those who have served us LONG *and* FAITHFULLY. "Reckon," says Mr. Janeway, " that one who has been a faithful servant to you seven years, deserves to be esteemed next to a child ever after." Tried fidelity should be marked with peculiar approbation. At the end of each seven years of faithful service you should present them with some substantial present, as a token of your respect and gratitude, and the present should increase in value at the close of each septennial period. Where there is wealth to be disposed of by will, I think that aged and valuable servants should be remembered. Think how much you owe to their faithfulness, how long your property has been in their power, which they have neither embezzled nor wasted, how constantly you have been served by them, how much they have contributed to your domestic comfort, perhaps, to your success. You owe them not only wages but esteem.

Thirdly. But there are duties of a still higher and more sacred character, owed by you to your servants, I mean those of RELIGION.

They have souls as well as you; like you, are immortal creatures; like you, are sinners; and like you, the objects of redeeming mercy. The very circumstance of their being brought within the comprehension of your domestic circle, has made them a part of that little community, the spiritual welfare of which you are to promote and to watch with all possible solicitude. They are members of the domestic constitution, as well as hired servants. We surely cannot suppose, that the fine and extensive power, which is lodged by the family compact in the master's hand, was vested there for so trivial a purpose as the mere payment of those wages, and the affording of that sustenance, which are necessary for supplying the servant's bodily wants. It is also to be recollected, *that moral duties are required from servants, and ought therefore to be taught.* With what propriety can we look for truth, honesty, temperance, chastity, if we have never inculcated these virtues? How can we expect they will be faithful in serving *us,* if we have never taught them *to serve God* in sincerity and truth?

1. Our first care must be not to *oppose their religion,* or *to hinder* their salvation. We may do this by the influence of a bad example. In what a heathenish state do some families live! Heathenish? No: for pagans have their household deities, and make some shew of religion, though it be a false one, in their houses: but great multitudes in this christian land, live as if there were no God, and are to all intents and purposes practical atheists. There is no family prayer,

no reading of the scriptures, no observance of the sabbath, no regular attendance upon public worship. The holy day of rest is to them as other days; they keep the same company, and seek the same recreations then as at any time besides. Religion is rarely introduced, but to be an object of contempt, and a source of ridicule. The servants in such families hear swearing perhaps; but no prayer; see drunkenness, but no worship; witness card playing, dancing, and conviviality, but no acknowledgment of God. How can such masters expect good servants? If *they* habitually break *God's* commands, how can they expect their servants to keep theirs? Unreasonable men, can you look for sobriety in them, if you set them the example of intoxication? For chastity, if you teach them lewdness? For truth, if you teach them falsehood? For religion, if you teach them irreligion? O that you would consider that your wickedness ensures not only your own damnation, but hazards that of all the persons under your charge. Is it not enough to have your own sins laid to your charge, but that you must be answerable for your servant's sins also? Is one curse too light, but you must seek to multiply it? Are the flames of hell so cool and tolerable, that you are busy in adding fuel to that terrible fire, to make it burn seven times hotter? Yours will not be the privilege of perishing alone, but will be the fate of the pilot, who sinks others with himself.

Some carry the matter so far, as to *hinder* the salvation of others, not only by *example*, but by DIRECT

TEMPTATION. How many masters have by their atrocious and murderous arts, corrupted the virtue, blasted the reputation, and ruined the souls of those females, whom, having received into their house, they were bound, by every principle of honour, as well as of religion, to protect. Such wretches deserve the gallows far more than many who suffer there. How many poor unhappy women have been sent by such vile transgressors, into the career of prostitution, to an early grave, and to that place of punishment, where they will meet their seducer to be his tormentor, through eternity. Neither a word, nor a look, should ever be given to a servant, which has the remotest tendency to injure her modesty.

Nor ought you to tempt them to sin, *by employing them to practice dishonesty and falsehood in the way of trade.* Do not engage them in acts of fraud upon the revenue; nor make them the spectators of your own evasion of the laws which regulate the taxes; for all such conduct as this, is laying a snare in their way, and tempting them to sin. And by what sophistry can any one attempt to justify that wicked practice of *commanding their servants to say to visitors, that they are* NOT AT HOME, *while they are in the house at the very time?* This is teaching falsehood by system, and ought we to wonder if our servants should lie *to* us, when we have thus taught them to lie *for* us? People that make any profession of religion, cannot, of course, adopt this iniquitous custom, for it disgraces the most *general* acknowledgment of piety: but it is to be feared that some, who pass for real christians, and wish to be thought such, are guilty of many things which are quite unworthy of their character, in reference to their servants, either by making them the witnesses or instruments of many evasions, artifices, and dishonourable acts; and by which they really tempt them to go much farther astray on their own account. We can easily conceive, with what insufferable loathing and disgust some such servants must come to the domestic altar, at the time of the morning or evening sacrifice. It is a most shocking instance of hypocrisy when a master says to his servants, "After you have done so and so,"—(alluding to some act of imposition upon others)—" come to prayer." " Come to prayer," one might imagine they reply, "thou hypocrite, what to sanctify the dishonesty thou has just commanded us to perform? Many who have witnessed these things, or any thing like them, have taken an inveterate prejudice against religion, by concluding, that all its professors are alike, and that all are hypocrites together.

We *hinder* their salvation, *when we keep them away from the means of grace.* Their work should not be so oppressive even on week days, as to allow them no time for reading the scriptures and prayer; but to compel them to spend even their Sabbaths in such a manner as to deprive them of opportunity to hear the word of God explained and enforced, by the faithful preaching of the gospel, is to place a most powerful hindrance in the way of their salvation. How exceedingly cruel and disgraceful is it to keep them from public worship to dress a warm dinner. Without affirming that the christian Sabbath is to be observed with the same ceremonial strictness as the Jewish Sabbath was, we do contend, that no *unnecessary* work should be done on that day in our dwellings. I suppose no one will contend that a *warm* dinner is necessary. Is it not a crime, then, against the spiritual welfare of our servants, as well as against God, to occupy *their* sabbath in preparing for our luxurious gratification? Even as it respects their bodies, it is an act of great oppression, for *they* need rest from their labours far more than we do: and as it respects their souls, it takes away both the opportunity and the inclination to attend to these: it occupies their time in the morning, and unfits them for attention in the afternoon. All who thus employ their domestics on the Sabbath, may be truly said to feast upon their servant's birth-right, and to gratify *their* palate at the expense of their fellow creatures' spiritual and eternal welfare. How long and how loudly shall the voice of indignant and faithful reprobation be raised in vain against this sinful practice? I put it to any professing christians's conscience, how he can any longer determine thus to hinder the salvation of those who are under his care? Will he not make even *this* small sacrifice for the spiritual welfare of the members of his domestic constitution? Is *this* his professed zeal for God, and compassion for souls? But, perhaps, he will reply, some body must be at home to guard the house. Be it so. But need they be slavishly occupied in the drudgery of cookery? If they must be deprived of the *public* means of grace, is it necessary that they should be deprived of those that are private also? But they will not improve their time at home. How do you know? Have you tried them? Have you, before you left home, furnished them with a suitable portion of reading.

In some families, the servants are kept away from the house of God far more than they need to be, for other purposes besides cooking. If there are two children, one must be detained from public worship for each, and perhaps a third to guard the house. But is this necessary? I would have all proper care taken, both of the children, and of the property; but I would not have more servants than are absolutely requisite, kept away from the house of God. The Sabbath is of more importance to them than it is even to us. Their incessant occupation through the week, renders it more necessary for *them* to have a day of rest and of leisure to attend to their souls' concerns, than it is for us. Nor do I think it enough to grant them merely the afternoon of the Lord's day; for that is the very part of the Sabbath, which we find to be the least edifying to ourselves, and if this be the case with us, how much more so must it be with them? If then, we keep away our servants from suitable public means of grace, we are placing a hindrance in the way of their salvation; for we know that " faith cometh by hearing, and hearing by the word of God;" and that

God hath ordained the *preaching* of the gospel for the salvation of men's souls.

It appears to me, that we tempt our servants to sin also, *by improper negligence and carelessness about many of the more covetable parts of our property.* Some persons are too much away from home, and leave their servants too much to themselves; and when *they* are idle abroad, is it any wonder that their domestics should be dishonest at home? If *they* will gossip away their time by hours, and days, and weeks together, can it be wondered at, that their property should be wasted by those who are only *hired* to watch it? If *you* are so much from home, is it not a temptation to *them* to invite company? Is this habit of neglecting them the way to make them faithful? Will they not learn idleness from you, and do you not know that idleness is a parent sin? Or if you tempt them not to sin by being too much from home, do you not do it by giving them *too little employment?* If you overwork them, you oppress their bodies; if you underwork them, you endanger their souls. It is said of the wise and virtuous woman, that she would suffer none of her household to eat the bread of idleness. You must account, not only for your own time, but for theirs also. When your servants are idle, said an old author, the devil is at work; and our idle days are his busy ones: if you find them nothing to do, he will. Many have been ruined for both worlds, by having nothing to do—but mischief. Do not tempt them to sin, by *never calling them to account* for what is entrusted to their care;

especially in pecuniary matters. They may be honest; then keep them so, and put no temptation in their way to be otherwise, by not examining their accounts. Never let them feel that they are irresponsible. If you keep not your eye upon them you may find a thief where you expected to find an honest man. It is your prayer for yourself, "lead me not into temptation;" act upon this same principle towards them. Honesty itself should always be required to account for the uttermost farthing, and will wish to do it. Do not leave your property too much exposed. Some go to one extreme, and lock up every thing, others go to the opposite extreme, and lock up nothing; and here, as in many other cases, extremes meet, for one tempts to dishonesty by trusting too little, the other by trusting too much. Money, drinkables, and the lighter articles of female dress and decoration, should not be left too carelessly about. Nor should one party in married life, ever make a confederacy with servants to deceive the other. Wives should never engage their maids in a scheme of falsehood, imposition, or concealment of any kind against their husbands, though it be but in trifling matters, for this is teaching them intrigue and duplicity, which may not only be injurious to their own character, but seriously detrimental in the end to the interests of the family. If a servant be employed by the wife, to assist her to conceal any part of the husband's property, or appropriate it in any way unknown to him, she is in that act tempted by her mistress, so far as the influence of example goes, to take the same liberty on her own account; for she who is employed to purloin for another, will soon feel no scruples to steal for herself.

2. It is our duty, not only not to *hinder* the salvation of our servants, but *to do every thing in our power to promote it.*

Seriously consider your obligation in this particular; and that as God sent them under your roof, that you might care for their souls, so HE WILL REQUIRE THEIR SOULS AT YOUR HANDS. Yes, at the day of judgment he will say to you, " Give an account of those immortal beings which were placed under your instruction, inspection, and anxiety." Cherish, then, I entreat you, a deep solicitude for their spiritual welfare, and feel desirous to become the instruments of their salvation. In order to this, take care to set them a good example, and let them see in you, not only nothing that is contrary to religion, but every thing that can recommend it, that so an attractive influence may ever be exerted by your character on theirs. Many have learnt more of religion by what they have seen in their masters and mistresses, than by all they have heard from their ministers. They will never forget their example. Call them regularly to family prayer, and make them the peculiar subjects of your earnest supplications, that they may hear your entreaties with God on their account, and be the witnesses of your solicitude for their welfare. See to it that they have bibles, and take care that they are able to read, for if this be not the case, it is your bounden duty to teach them. Furnish them with a few well selected books, and thus provide for them a kitchen library. Give them opportunities to attend public worship, and to keep holy the Sabbath day. Keep them not too late at work on Saturday evening, lest their worldly business trench upon the Sabbath, or unfit them by excessive fatigue, for its hallowed occupations. Instruct them in the principles of true religion, that they may have their judgments rightly informed, and that they may not perish for lack of knowledge. It is a great disgrace to a christian master or mistress, if any servants leave their house, without knowing, at least in theory, the way of salvation. In addition to this, you should talk to them in the most affectionate manner on their souls' concerns, warning them to flee from the wrath to come, and directing them to the Lamb of God, which taketh away the sin of the world. Give them no rest till you have prevailed upon them to seek in good earnest, the one thing needful. Observe what company they keep, and caution them against such as would lead them astray. Acquaint yourselves with the books they read, and examine what they understand and remember of the sermons they hear. Do all you can to convince them of the reasonableness, profit, and sweetness of true religion, and of the folly, and danger, and misery of living without it. If you see no fruit of your exertions at first, do not be weary of well doing, but persevere in your anxious and judicious efforts. Should you notice any solicitude about their souls, nourish to the uttermost their impressions by giving suitable advice and proper books. Encourage them, when you are convinced of their true conversion, to connect themselves with the church of Christ, and thus to make a public profession of religion. O, if you should be the instrument of saving the souls of your servants, what an honour and a happiness will be conferred upon you! How many *have been* so honoured; and in what bonds have their servants been held to them for ever after in this life.

To influence you to the performance of these duties, I may call upon you, *to remember that your Master also is in heaven,* and *to consider what a master he is to you.* Meditate upon his attributes, and upon the manner in which they are manifested in all his conduct towards you. How righteous, how faithful, how holy, how true, how merciful is he in *his* dealings towards *his* servants. And it is your duty to be like him. When in danger of acting improperly, either by a want of equity or kindness, O think of God; meditate on his matchless grace, and surely such a reflection will be an immediate check to every kind, and every degree of impropriety. To him also you are accountable, and accountable, as for your conduct in general, so also for your behaviour to your servants. Prepare to meet Him in that awful day, and to meet them also at his bar!!

Consider *how much your servants need this kind interposition for their welfare.* They are often young, inexperienced, and ignorant; rash, and imprudent; and they are also an unprotected and dependent race. I know not a class of persons whose situation is more calculated to awaken our tenderest sympathies, than domestic female servants. Many of them are orphans, and have no friend in the world, beyond their employers; and no home but what they find in their master's house. When they leave one place of service, they often know not where to find their next home, and are thus repeatedly beginning the world, and setting out on the journey of life afresh. How many dangers are they exposed to! How many snares are laid for their feet! Masters and mistresses, be kind to them; they have found a refuge in your house, and let them find friends in you. Pity their condition, and labour to the uttermost for their welfare. You may be the means of blessing them for both worlds, and become their spiritual fathers and mothers, as well as their temporal masters and mistresses. Their souls may be given to your kind solicitude, to be your crown of rejoicing in the day of eternity.

The honour of religion is most deeply involved in the way in which you discharge your duties. Bad masters and mistresses bring great dishonour upon christianity; while on the other hand, they who in this situation, exhibit whatsoever things are pure, and true, and honest, and just, and lovely, and of good report; who abound in that love which is not easily provoked, and thinketh no evil, and is kind; who have the meekness and gentleness of Christ; and who put on bowels of mercy, are bright ornaments of their profession, and adorn the doctrine of God their Saviour in all things. *A good master or mistress* is indeed a most honourable character; good men esteem it, bad men admire it, the world values it, the church applauds it, angels delight in it, and God commends and rewards it. Eyes too dim to see the beauties of holiness in the abstract, discern the excellence of this, and tongues that never speak of religion generally, but to scoff at it, are eloquent in the praise of this. I conjure you, then, by all the regard you bear to the honour of religion, strive to excel in this your appropriate duty.

Interest pleads with you for this. Consider how much your own happiness will be promoted, by seeing others happy around you. The heart of that man cannot be in the state in which it ought to be, who is not pleased to see around him in his dwelling, a circle of happy minds and smiling countenances. A good master, or a kind mistress, is a kind of central luminary in the domestic system, and every child and every servant an attendant satellite, revolving in the force of his attraction, and reflecting the brightness of his glory. Or to change the metaphor, he is a fountain of gladness, continually sending forth in kindness and kind actions, streams of pleasure to all that are in the house. And then good masters or mistresses *make* good servants or *find* them. When I hear persons complain, that they cannot find good servants, I suspect the fault is their own, and that they have a bad character for their conduct towards their domestics. If they are tormented, have they not been tormentors? If they can get no one to serve them willingly, and honestly, have they been generous and kind? If they find none but such as are wicked, have they tried to make them holy? If they complain of their lying, their lewdness, their theft, have they not been so selfish as to seek or to produce right dispositions towards themselves, without endeavouring to found these dispositions on a right state of mind towards God? Try, then, to conduct yourselves rightly to those, whom you have so much interest in making what they should be. Body, soul, estate, wife, children, character, comfort, all are more or less concerned in this matter. Your servants may rob or enrich you; may defend your reputation, or blast it; may corrupt your children, or improve them: may tempt you to sin, or warn you against it; may injure your health or protect it; may bless you by their prayers, or curse you by their vices; may render your dwelling continually pleasant, or perpetually miserable: your own interest, therefore, unites with God's commands, to make it your wisdom and your duty, to train your servants as well as your children in the fear of the Lord.

"What have you to say against what I have been persuading you to? Will you not now, without delay bewail your former neglect, and in good earnest set to your work, like persons that in some measure know the power of divine precepts, the worth of souls, and the greatness of the charge that lieth upon you? O that there were in you such a heart. O that all masters of families were resolved for that which humanity, reason, interest, reputation, and their comfort call for, as well as the law of God, and men oblige them to. What blessed families then should we have! What noble corporations! What glorious cities! Might not HOLINESS TO THE LORD, be written upon every door? O, when shall it once be."

CHAPTER IX.

THE DUTIES OF SERVANTS.

"Servants be obedient unto them that are your masters, according to the flesh, with fear and trembling, in singleness of your heart, as unto Christ; not with eye service, as men pleasers; but as the servants of Christ, doing the will of God from the heart; with good will, doing service, as to the Lord, and not to men: knowing that whatsoever good thing any man doeth, the same shall he receive of the Lord, whether it be bond or free."
EPHESIANS, vi. 5—8.

"Honour and shame from no condition rise,
"Act well your part—there all the honour lies."

GOD is the Creator of all things and the disposer of all events; he is, therefore, the author of all those varieties which are to be found in nature, and of all those differences which exist in society. He that formed the sun to illuminate, and to rule, formed also the planets to be enlightened and to be governed; and he that raiseth the king to the throne, ordaineth the lot of the servants in the house, and of the labourer in the field. There is no such thing as chance; no not in the material universe, where each bird that flies, each insect that crawls, each flower that blooms, amidst the desert, which man's eye never explores, is the separate production of divine power and skill, no less than the alpine height that lifts its snow-crowned summit to the skies, and receives the admiring contemplation of millions. Nor is there any such thing as chance in society ; the rank and station of the poor little servant girl in the humblest dwelling of the most obscure village, are as certainly determined by God, as the elevation of the conqueror and ruler of nations. " The lot is cast into the lap, but the disposal thereof is from the Lord." "The rich and the poor meet together, but the Lord is the disposer of them all ;" i. e. not simply their Creator, as men, but the disposer of their circumstances, as rich and poor. This is comforting, this is reconciling. It prevents the poor from being degraded in their own eyes, or in the eyes of others. They are not like the dust, or the chips, or the dried and withered leaves in autumn, which, amidst the more stately objects of nature and art, are blown about by the gusts which sweep along the surface ; but they are in the place which God intended for them ; and God hath made every thing beautiful in its place and season. Who could have mended what he hath done ? What cause have we to sit down contented, and thankful, in the place which he hath ordained for us! What obligation was he under to give us existence ? And what did he owe to us that he should have made us rational creatures, and not formed us a beast, or a reptile ? "Shall the thing formed, say to him that formed it, Why hast thou made me thus ?"

As God disposeth every thing, so it is the highest

excellence of a creature, to discharge the duties of his station, and to shine in the orbit, and move with regularity through the course allotted to him. A good servant is more honourable than a bad master; and a valuable subject than a worthless prince. He that is not *relatively* good, is not *really* so; while he that acts *his* part well, is more truly dignified, though his rank be low, than he that stands on a pinnacle, but fails in the duty of his elevated station. What is true honour? Not riches, not rank, not beauty, not learning, not courage. No. But virtue; whether it be clad in the garb of poverty, or the robe of affluence; whether it hold the plough, or grasp the sceptre; whether it be seated at the table, or stand behind the chair. VIRTUE IS HONOUR; let all servants write this sentimeet on the heart, and ever act under its influence, as the living principle of all their conduct.

In stating, after these preliminary remarks, the duties of servants, I would remind them.

First. *That there are some which they owe* TO THEMSELVES, the performance of which will constitute the best and surest foundation of those which they owe to others.

1. RELIGION takes the lead of all.

Religion is as much your business, as it is ours. You are immortal creatures, you are sinners, you are the objects of God's mercy, in Christ Jesus, and invited to seek pardon, peace, and eternal life, as well as we your employers. You have souls that must suffer eternal torments in hell, or enjoy everlasting happiness in heaven. You must be convinced of sin, repent, confess to God, cry for mercy, commit your souls into the hands of Christ by faith, be born again of the Holy Ghost, lead a sober, righteous, and godly life, or you must depart accursed into everlasting fire, prepared for the devil and his angels. God is as willing to have mercy upon you; Jesus Christ is as ready to receive you as he is us. Your soul is as precious in the eye of heaven as ours. God is no respecter of persons, and is not to be considered as less friendly to your best interests, because he has placed you in service. *Your situation is no excuse, therefore, for your neglecting the claims of religion.* You are not to imagine that attention to your soul's concerns is not required from *you*, for it is required; and I repeat it, unless you repent, and are born again, and believe in Christ, *you* will perish eternally. Your soul is your first concern, and must not be neglected for any thing. Think not that it is impossible for a person in your situation to attend to religion; for *it* is possible. Great multitudes of servants, both male and female, are truly pious. I have twenty or thirty in the church under my care, who are among its most consistent members. I charge you all, to live in the fear of God. Remember your Creator. Set the Lord always before you. Consider that he is ever about your path, and that you act, speak, and think in his presence. He is now the holy and ever present witness, and will hereafter be the inflexible judge of your actions.

In order to cultivate religion, go not into wicked families, where the sabbath is profaned, the claims of piety despised and rejected, and you can have no opportunity of going to public worship. Do not dwell in a place where your sabbath is taken away from you; let no amount of wages tempt you to go to, or to remain in such a situation. Always stipulate for the privilege of going at least one part of the Lord's day, to the house of God. Insist upon it as your right, and suffer nothing to deprive you of it. Endeavour to find a little time for reading the bible, and for prayer. Never go out of your room in the morning, nor lie down on your pillow at night, without reading a portion, even though it be a short one, of God's holy word, and earnestly praying for his mercy. Let religion be the basis of all your conduct, the very framework of your character, leading you to practice " whatsoever things are true, whatsoever things are honest, whatsoever things are just, and pure, and lovely, and of good report." Do not, then, as you would escape the torments of hell, do not, as you would be brought at last to the felicities of heaven, DO NOT NEGLECT YOUR SOULS. " Godliness is profitable for all things, having the promise of the life that now is, as well as of that which is to come." Your situation is a very dangerous one; you are in a very unprotected state: and you need the fear of God to enable you to depart from evil. Men, and women too, of bad principles, are lying in wait for you, spreading snares for your feet, and seeking your ruin. Religion will guard you, and guide you, and comfort you; it will keep you in safety, and raise you to respectability. "Exalt her, and she shall promote thee, she shall lead thee to honour when thou dost embrace her."

2. A REGARD TO TRUTH, is another very important duty, and which you will be sure to perform if you fear God. This duty you owe to your employers also; but while the *inconvenience* of the neglect of it will be felt by them, the more dreadful consequence of that neglect will be yours.

Lying is a most hateful and wicked practice. And it is said, that " all liars shall have their portion in the lake that burneth with fire." Strive to avoid every thing in your conduct, that needs a lie to cover it; but if you have at any time done any thing wrong, do not make one sin two, by telling a falsehood to conceal the matter. Let no temptation induce you to violate truth, rather endure the passion, or the bitterest wrath of the severest master or mistress, than strive to avert it by a falsehood. Lying is bad policy, as well as great wickedness; for, when once detected in this vice, you will ever afterwards be suspected, even when you tell the truth. A servant, whose word can be implicitly relied upon, will always be esteemed. Such a virtue will be made to extend a friendly covering over many little faults. Never allow yourselves to be tempted by your master or mistress, to commit a breach of truth. Inform them at once, that they must tell their own falsehoods, for that you cannot do it for them. A clerk once waited upon me, to ask me what he was to do in a situation, where he was obliged weekly to make a false written return in his own name, to defraud a public company, for the benefit of his employer. "Do," said I, with surprise that the question should have been asked me, "instantly refuse; and rather cast yourself and your family the next hour upon Providence, than ever repeat the falsehood." You must not, dare not, lie for others, any more than for yourselves. If required to adopt the modern practice of saying your mistress is not at home, when she is at the same time in the house; you dare not comply, for it is a falsehood, and as such, a sin against God. When you are put by your employers upon committing any sin, whether it be cheating, calumny, lying, or any thing else forbidden by the scriptures, let your reply be, "How can I do this great wickedness, and sin against God?"

3. SOBRIETY is a virtue you owe to yourselves, and also to your masters: but, as in the case of lying, the injury done by intoxication to yourselves, is far greater than that which you inflict upon them.

Beware of the besotting, impoverishing, debasing sin of drunkenness, and of every thing that leads to it. Household servants have many opportunities, and many temptations to practice this vice, if there be any propensity to indulge in it. It is impossible even for the most rigid watchfulness always to keep out of their reach the malt liquor, the spirits, and the wine; there are means of gaining access by stealth to these things, on the part of a vicious and ingenious servant, which no vigilant mistress can altogether prevent. If we cannot trust these things to the guardianship of your principles, our locks and keys will often be found an insufficient security. Do, do consider, that if the habit of drunkenness be once contracted, it is all over; and most probably you are ruined for both worlds. Let there be a distinct understanding between you and your master or mistress, what beverage you are to be allowed, both as to quality and quantity, and most sacredly abstain from touching a drop more, or a drop of any thing else. Never put the decanters to your lips, when the stoppers are all out before you. Stolen drams of this kind, are double poison, they are venom for the body, and damnation for the soul; they lead to two crimes at once, drunkenness and dishonesty. Beware of the temptation which is presented at those times, when company is in the house, and when, through the supposition that extra exertion requires an additional glass, you may be led to take it, to love it, and to acquire the *habit* of it. I have known excellent servants, both male and female, ruined for ever by intoxication.

As to workmen, the daily servants that occupy the manufactories, this vice is the damning sin that is spreading immorality, desolation, and misery through almost the whole labouring classes of the community. It is distressing, beyond the power of language to describe, to think of the effects of this most prevalent, most dreadful infatuation. How many fine, athletic forms are enervated; how many wives are broken hearted; how many families are reduced to beggary; how many souls are damned continually, by this crime. Drunken servants are the torment of almost all our master manufacturers, the curse upon our commerce, and the blight upon our national prosperity.

4. CHASTITY is a duty of infinite importance to the well being of servants.

I am now on delicate ground, and I will endeavour to step with caution : but no false refinement shall hinder me from discharging a duty, which, as a guardian of the public morals, I owe to a very large, and a very much exposed class of my fellow creatures. I will not allow a prudish and effected sentimentalism to turn away my holy and benevolent concern from the interests of female servants, nor prevent me from addressing to them the language of warning and expostulation. When the miseries of prostitution are considered, and when the prevalence of this desolating crime, and all its attendant evils is at once admitted and deplored; when it is well known, that of the miserable and loathsome victims of seduction that crowd the paths of vice, a very large proportion were female servants, betrayed from the ways of virtue, in the first instance, by their masters, or their masters' sons, or their fellow servants of the opposite sex, surely it is the duty of every one who is specially addressing young women in service, most solemnly and most pointedly to warn them against the wily arts of the basilisk seducer, who is fascinating them to their ruin. Young women, consider the value, even in this world, of your character. With an unblemished reputation, you are respectable in servitude : your virtue is your parents' honest boast, your families' only renown, and your own wealth and honour : this will be your passport through the world, your letter of recommendation to good society, and that which will find you friends, and make them, and keep them, wherever Providence may cast your lot. But if this be lost, oh, what a poor, forlorn, withered, wretched creature you become ; abandoned by your seducer, ejected from your place, disowned by your friends, you have the pains, and the cares, and the labours of a mother, but united with the infamy of a prostitute ; you have to bear from without the scorn of the world, the look and language of shame-stricken, heart-broken parents, and the ceaseless reproach and remorse of a guilty conscience from within; and all this, perhaps, but as preliminary to the misery which the prostitute endures, through her loathsome course on earth, and its awful termination in hell. Take warning, then, and reject with disdain and virtuous indignation, the very first encroachments that may be made, by any one, upon the most delicate modesty and reserve. Have you been unfortunate enough to draw upon yourself the attention of a master, or a master's son, consider, it is with the eye of lust, not of love, that he looks upon you; he may flatter your vanity by his admiration of your person, but it is the flattery of a murderer; he cannot mean any thing that is honourable; his passion, that he talks of, is a base, ruffian-like, deliberate purpose to ruin you. Turn from him, flee from him with more haste than you would from a serpent or a tiger, for more than a serpent or a tiger is he to be shunned by you. Make him feel that you are his superior in virtue, though his inferior in rank. If, on the other hand, you allow him to accomplish his purpose, and decoy you to perdition, he will in cold-blooded, remorseless cruelty, abandon you and your child to a workhouse, to a broken heart, and the bottomless pit.

Act in the same determined manner towards every one else. Preserve not only your virtue itself, but your modesty, which is its outwork. Allow neither act, nor word, nor look, in your presence, which is at variance with the most scrupulous purity. Let no prospect, nor promise of marriage, throw you off your guard. The man who acts thus, is to be regarded as a traitor, deceiving you into iniquity. He that would destroy your reputation, will not scruple to falsify his own word; the vows of such a wretch are not to be trusted. Be careful to whom you give your company. Let not an anxiety to leave service, and be your own mistress, drive you to accept the offer of the first individual, without considering whether he be suitable or unsuitable, who may present himself to your notice.

5. FRUGALITY is an incumbent duty upon persons in your situation.

You are in very dependant circumstances. Your support depends upon your own labour, and that upon your health. You have no arm but your own to rely upon, and should therefore feel the obligation of laying up something in the day of prosperity, against the night of adversity. We are all enjoined to *trust* Providence, but not to *tempt* it. To spend all we get in vanity and useless trifles, under the idea that we shall be taken care of, in one way or other, is a presumption that generally brings its own punishment. There is in the present day, a most censurable propensity in female servants, and workwomen in general, to dress quite beyond their station. It is not easy, in some cases, to distinguish between the maid and her mistress. What abject folly is it, for a young woman to spend all her wages in gay apparel. When she is in ill health and out of place, will it be any consolation to look upon finery which she is obliged to pawn, one article after another, for her support? The love of dress has led in some instances to stealing; in others, to prostitution; in more, to poverty. Character is respectability, not dress. Harlots are generally fine and gaudy in their attire. Economize your little property, then; lay up in store for the time to come. I know several servants who have, one forty, another fifty, another one hundred pounds in the bank. Besides, it is desirable to save from unnecessary expence in dress, that you may have a little to give to the cause of humanity and religion. The mite of the servant may mingle, in this age, with the pound of the master, to help in spreading the blessings of christianity over the face of the earth. And it is to be poor indeed, to have nothing to give to the cause of humanity or religion.

Secondly. I now lay before you, *the duties you owe to* YOUR EMPLOYERS.

1. *Honour them,* for they are your superiors in station. Pay them the respect which is due to them; and in order to this, cherish for them a proper reverence in your heart. " Let as many servants as are under the yoke," said the apostle, " count their own masters worthy of all honour." Behave towards them with all proper humility and submission: not that you are to crouch and tremble before them, like slaves at the foot of a tyrant. Your address to them must be reverential, not rude, boisterous, and impertinent. In talking of them to others, in their absence, there should be no calling them names, no exposure of their faults, no ridiculing their infirmities; on the contrary, you should, to the utmost of your power, as far as truth will allow, defend them against the attacks of slander, and the arts of detraction. If at any time, they speak to you with tones of anger, and in language of rebuke, you must remember the apostle's injunction, and " not *answer again.*" You may mildly and meekly explain, and sometimes expostulate, but you must not reply in an angry and impertinent manner. Should they so far forget their duty, as to let down their dignity, and be too familiar, do not forget *your* place, but respectfully keep your proper distance. Every thing rude in conduct, and obtrusive, insolent or familiar in language, must, therefore, be most sedulously avoided, as an essential part of servants' conduct towards their employers.

2. OBEDIENCE is founded upon reverence, and is a necessary part of it. Observe the directions of the apostle Paul:—" Servants, *obey in all things* your masters according to the flesh." We are of course to except those things which are contrary to the word of God; for if they enjoin any thing that is manifestly sinful, you must mildly, but firmly, refuse to comply, and be prepared to take all the consequences of your disobedience. In all other matters, however self-denying or difficult, however contrary to your own views and wishes, you must submit; you are not to choose your commands, but in all things to obey. You are to obey " *with fear and trembling,*" i. e. with reverential regard for their authority, a dread of their displeasure, and also, which is probably the apostle's meaning, with a dread of the anger of God, who, having enjoined obedience, will punish the disobedient. You are to obey in " *singleness of heart,*" i. e. with a willing and cheerful mind; and not with a mere compulsory outside shew of submission, and are to be free from all selfish personal ends, and obey from the single consideration, that it is right. You are to do this, " *as unto Christ, as the servants of Christ, doing the will of God from the heart, with good will, doing service as to the Lord, and not to men.*" You must consider that God commands it, and therefore you are to obey them, as obeying God; they are in God's stead, in this particular, to you; and from a regard to conscience, and a respect to the divine authority, you are to do what they enjoin. "I do this," you are to say,

in reference to obedience, "not *merely* to please my master and my mistress, but to please God." This is turning all you do into religion. It signifies nothing, what is the nature of the thing, whether it be an act of the most menial kind, in the kitchen, the parlour, or the garden, if it be done with a view to the divine command, that very aim elevates the humble service into an expression of piety towards God, and a service that will be remembered in the day of judgment. You are not to obey, "*with eye service, as men pleasers.*" How many are there, who need a master's eye always upon them, to keep them industrious. No sooner is his back turned, than they are indolent and neglectful. This conduct is as mean as it is wicked: it is detestable hypocrisy, flagrant injustice, and manifest wickedness: for is it nothing that the eye of God is upon you? Is he not there? Does he not disapprove this conduct? And is it a small matter to make light of *his* presence? Such servants will shortly find, to their fearful cost, that the eye of God is far more to be dreaded, than the eye of the severest master.

Let it be your *delight* to do the will of your employers. Strive to please them in all things, and feel anxious to draw from them this testimony.—" There is a servant, to whom no command, which it is in her power to obey, comes unwelcome; who never need be told a second time to do a thing; who anticipates my orders; and whose very pleasure seems to arise from pleasing me."

3. Good temper, is of great consequence.

There are some servants who, let what work will come in unexpectedly, and even oppressively, receive all with a cheerful acquiescence, and are never put out of their way. Their mistresses are never afraid of telling them of unlooked for company having arrived, and extra exertion being necessary. While there are others, who, with many valuable qualities, are withal so peevish, so soon put out of temper, so cross at any little unexpected addition being made to their work, that their mistresses are in constant bondage. I like not to hear it said, " She is a very good servant, and has many excellent properties, but her temper is so bad, that I am quite afraid to point out to her, in ever so gentle a manner, the least imperfection, or to put her in the smallest degree out of her way." This is a serious blemish upon any excellence, and often proves a very great interruption to the comfort of the family, but a still greater interruption to the comfort of the poor waspish creature herself. Temper is not every thing, but it is very important. Study, therefore, to be obliging, and to avoid crossness, sullenness, and passion.

4. FIDELITY is a duty of the *highest rank*.

What a delightful testimony is that which our Lord Jesus Christ is represented as bearing to his people at the last day,—" *Well done, good and* FAITHFUL *servant.*" Such also is the testimony, which it should be in our power to bear to our servants. Fidelity has reference—

To the property of your masters.

Faithful servants will not STEAL the property of their masters. There are opportunities of this every where if you choose to avail yourselves of them. Consider the horrible disgrace of being called a thief; and add to this, the danger in the present world, and the punishment of such a crime in the next. Write the eighth commandment upon your heart, and when tempted by a favourable opportunity to embezzle the property of your employer, let a voice more awful than thunder, repeat in your ears the prohibition, " Thou shalt not steal." At that perilous moment in your history, let your imagination look up, and behold the flaming eye of God intently gazing upon you. In whatever profusion, money, plate, jewellery, lace, may be spread out before you, touch not, covet not. Determine, by God's grace, that though you be ever so poor, you will, at least, be honest. Honesty is indeed the best policy, to go no higher for a motive and commendation. A single act of stealing may blast your reputation for ever: even to be suspected, is dreadful: but what inestimable value is attached to a servant of tried honesty. Be honest even to *scrupulosity*. Touch nothing in the house in the way of *eatables* or *drinkables*, which you do not consider as belonging to you. If you want to taste the luxuries of the larder, ask for them; but do not appropriate to yourself what you think would be denied. I have read of a servant who went into the pantry, only to make free with sweetmeats, but seeing some articles of plate lying about, he took these, and went on from one degree of theft to another, till he died at the gallows. He was under the influence of a thievish disposition when he saw the plate, for he was going to take what he had no right to, and he was in a favourable state of mind to be tempted by Satan to a greater crime. Servants should not allow themselves to appropriate any refuse articles of dress, nor give away the broken victuals, or other articles of the kitchen, without permission. Habits begin in acts; little sins lead on to greater ones. She that commences by taking a sweetmeat, knowing that she is not allowed it, has violated so far, her integrity; has done something to benumb her conscience, and has taken the first step towards confirmed dishonesty. Sin is deceitful; and the way of a sinner is like the course of a ball down hill. Servants, beware of the *first* act of sin. But fidelity, in reference to property, requires not only that you should not embezzle your master's property, but that you should not WASTE it. They that carelessly waste, are almost as guilty as they that wilfully steal. You cannot be an honest servant, unless you are as careful of your employer's property, as if it were your own. Furniture, goods, provisions, must all be thus preserved. You are not to say, " My master is rich, he can spare it, and we need not be so niggardly." His wealth is nothing to you; if *he* chooses to waste it, he has a legal right to do so, but you have none.

Nor is this all; for fidelity requires that servants *should do all they can to make their employers' affairs prosper.* They should grieve over their master's losses, rejoice in his success, and so identify their feelings with his interests, as to seem as if their fortune were bound up with his. We have a fine instance of this, in the case of Joseph while he was in the house of Potiphar.

Fidelity would also lead them to give their employers information and warning when their affairs are going wrong, either through their own neglect or ignorance, or through the injurious conduct of others. They cannot be honest, if they witness in silence any fraud practised upon them, either by their fellow servants, or by friends or strangers. Such connivance is a participation of the crime, although it should not be rewarded by any participation of the profits. A proper feeling of concern for your master's welfare would certainly lead you, if he were flagrantly neglectful of his affairs, to suggest to him, in a respectful manner, your apprehension of the consequences. What man, except a fool or a madman, would be offended by such an appeal as the following, made to him by a servant:—" Pardon me, sir, if I take the liberty of expressing my fears on the subject of your business, which I am induced to do, by a sense of my own duty, and a true regard to your welfare. Your business is certainly declining, and I fear, through your being so frequently absent from it. Customers are offended by not meeting with the principal in the shop, and by finding the stock so low and ill assorted. I am so concerned for your family, and so distressed at the idea of your doing otherwise than well, that at the risk of incurring your displeasure, which I entreat you not to indulge against me, for this self-denying act of faithful service, I have determined to lay the matter before you, and to beg you to give up your company, to look into your accounts, and to attend more closely to your business." A servant that would do this, and in this *manner*, is fidelity embodied, and is a treasure beyond all price.

But faithfulness has a reference also to a master's *time*, for in many instances, time is property, and servants may as effectually rob their masters by idleness, as by stealing. This is always the case where they are hired by the day; and indeed, where, as in many branches of manufacture, they are paid by the piece, if by their idleness they prevent their employers from executing orders, and realising profits, they can be scarcely called faithful. When you hire yourselves, there should be an explicit understanding, as I have already said, how much time you are to render for the stipulated wages, and when this is known, all that by indolence you keep back, is just so much of your employer's property stolen from him.

Faithfulness has regard to the *reputation* of your master and mistress. You have their character in your hands, and by calumny and falsehood, may, if such a malicious disposition were in your heart, do them considerable harm, either by stating what is absolutely false, misrepresenting what is true, magnifying what is little, or exaggerating what is insignificant. Remember, it is the utmost excess of base conduct, and the wickedest kind of dishonesty, to attempt to rob them of their good name.

Then there are also *secrets* which it would be a very unfaithful act in you to disclose. Workmen, clerks, and apprentices, are guilty of great impropriety, if they communicate the private arts of their master's business, or lay open his connexions to any one. Such an act is, by common opinion, an instance of criminal treachery. Female servants ought not to tell to others, what they see and hear in the families where they are placed. It is to be apprehended, that much of the gossip, and many of the reports, which circulate so much slander and detraction through society, are to be traced up to this source. You are not forbidden to form friendships with your fellow servants in other families, but to meet merely for the purpose of exchanging intelligence from the respective households in which you live, is highly censurable. You should maintain the strictest silence on these affairs, and not allow the most busy and inquisitive curiosity of others, to draw any thing from you. Nor are you to tell these matters, as is often done, *to one particular friend;* for she may tell them to one more, till at length the affairs of the family are matter of public notoriety. Your admission into a family is attended with an implied condition, that you are to keep all its secrets.

5. Diligence is another duty, but is so necessarily connected with honesty, and indeed, so essentially a part of it, that much need not be said, in addition, to

illustrate and enforce it. The slothful servant is a wicked one, for, in some instances, more mischief may be done by a day's idleness, than others may be able to undo by a year's exertion. The habits of a sluggard are very unfriendly to your own reputation, and to the comfort of the family by whom you are employed. *Early rising* is absolutely indispensable, if in addition to the duties of your station, you would attend to the salvation of your soul. And will you not sacrifice half an hour's sleep, for the purpose of seeking glory, honour, immortality, and eternal life? Diligence is opposed to sauntering, inactive, and gossiping habits; to a slow, reluctant, grudging, way of doing your work. A disposition to stint your labour, to do as little as you possibly can, and to do that little, in a careless, unneat, half-finished manner, is a great blemish in your character, and will be sure to militate against your interest.

6. GRATITUDE *for kindness shewn you,* is very incumbent.

You ought to be thankful for having your faults pointed out, and not resentful, as too many are, towards those who are kind enough to shew them what is wrong. If you have received kind attentions in sickness, and have discovered a constant solicitude on the part of your employers to soften as much as possible your labour, and to render you comfortable in your situation, you should convince them that their attentions are not thrown away upon one, who is insensible to their kindness. Especially, if they have taken pains to promote your interests, by warning you against bad company, or by endeavouring to correct your bad practices, you should be grateful for their pains, and endeavour to comply with their advice.

7. In all such cases as those mentioned, where your masters and mistresses are your friends, and confer obligations by their kindness, you should be *truly and cordially* ATTACHED *to them.*

Where there is really nothing to produce attachment, you cannot be expected to feel any. You cannot be required to feel gratitude, where you have received no favours; nor to cherish affection, where you have met with no indulgence. But *all* masters and mistresses are not tyrants, as some of you know by experience; for you have found in them, something. at least, of the kindness of a second father and mother. Here there are certainly strong claims upon your affection, and as they have cared for *you* with the kindness of parents, you should serve *them* with the deep interest and devoted attachment of children. They have a right to expect, in such instances, that as they have studied your comfort, you would study theirs; that when sickness invades their frame or their family, you will minister at the sick bed, by night or by day, not grudging your ease or your sleep, so that you might do them good; that when losses diminish their property or comforts, you will most tenderly sympathise with them, mingling your tears with theirs, and be willing to share with them the reduction of their usual plenty and gratification; that, in short, in all their afflictions, you will be afflicted with them, and be the sharers of all their joys. They did not, and they could not bargain with you for such a duty as this; affection cannot be made an article of money contract; it must be given, or it is worth nothing, and indeed, bought and sold it cannot be. Instances of a generous affection of this kind, we have perhaps all known; instances of servants so attached to their masters and mistresses, as to follow them, and remain in their service through all the vicissitudes of fortune; as to descend with them from the lofty eminence and luxurious gratifications of prosperity, down into the lowly and desolate, and barren vale of poverty, there to suffer want with them; as to leave their native land, and cross the seas, and dwell in a foreign country with them; as even to find in their love for their master and mistress, a principle and a feeling, that reconciled them to all the sufferings they endured on their account. I know a servant, who, when her master failed in business, brought down her little hoard of savings, amounting to nearly thirty pounds, and entreated him with tears to accept and apply it for the relief of his family. "Sir," said a lady to a minister who called upon her in sickness, "that girl," alluding to her servant, "who has just left the room, is a greater comfort to me than I can express. She watches me with the affection of a daughter, and the care of a nurse. When my complaints make me peevish, she contrives something to soothe me. I often observe her taking pains to discover what would add to my comfort, and often am presented with the thing I wish for, before I express it in words. I live without suspicion, for I perceive her to be conscientious, even to scrupulosity; my chief complaint is, that she takes so much care of me, that I cannot make her take sufficient care of herself."

Servants, look at this character, admire it, imitate it.

THIRDLY. *There are duties which servants in the same family owe* TO EACH OTHER.

There ought to be no *tyranny nor oppression exercised by one over the other.* This is often the case in those families which employ a numerous retinue of domestics, and which admit the distinction of superior and inferior servants. There is sometimes in such households, a system of great cruelty carried on altogether unknown to the master. Some poor creatures are degraded into the condition of a slave to the other servants, and drag on a miserable existence under the heavy yoke which has been imposed upon them, by an unfeeling minion, who stands before the master's eye, and has always his ear at command.

Strive to agree with each other, for families are often disturbed by the quarrels of the servants, and the uproar in the kitchen is distinctly heard by the guests in the parlour. You should bear with one another's infirmities, and never take delight in thwarting each other. Instead of finding pleasure in converting the infirmities of any one into a means of annoyance, and a source of vexation to her, carefully avoid whatever by appealing to these imperfections, or bringing them into notice, would render the subject of them irritable or sullen. Never tease one another, which is too often done, especially where an individual is known to be petulant. The worst consequences have sometimes arisen from this practice. A few days ago, I saw an individual put to the bar of his country, upon an indictment for manslaughter, under the following circumstances.—His fellow servants, aware of his petulant disposition, provoked him by some petty vexations, till, in his rage, he hurled a hammer at them, which struck one of them in the head, and inflicted a wound of which he died.

Never bear tales to your employers, for the purpose of exciting a prejudice against each other, and ingratiating yourselves in their favour. A supplanter is a most hateful character, at once despicable and despised.

At the same time, *you are not to connive at sin ;* if your fellow servants do any thing wrong, either in the way of drunkenness, lewdness, or dishonesty, you owe it to your master to make him acquainted with the fact. You are dishonest if you conceal the dishonesty of others, and you are a partaker of those vices which you allow to be perpetrated under your notice, without making it known.

Servants *that make a profession of religion* have great need to conduct themselves with singular propriety. Towards their masters and mistresses there should be the deepest humility, and the very reverse of every thing that bears even a distant resemblance of spiritual pride. There must be no consciousness of superiority, no air of importance, no affected sanctity; but a meek, modest, unobtrusive exhibition of the influence of religion, in making them strictly conscientious and exemplary in the discharge of all the duties of their station. Their piety should be seen, not only in a constant anxiety to attend to the public means of grace, and in a regular performance of the private duties of religion, but also in making them more respectful and obedient; more meek and submissive; more honest and diligent than all the rest. That servant does not adorn the doctrine of God her Saviour in all things, who does not shine in her sphere *as a servant.* There are occasions when you may seek to do good to those who employ you, if they are yet living without the possession of piety. Instances have occurred, in which, such as you have been the instruments of converting their employers: and a visible, but unostentatious exhibition of eminent and consistent piety, supported by as eminent a discharge of the duties of your station, followed by a modest and judicious introduction of the subject, when a suitable occasion presents itself, may, by the grace of God, be blessed for the salvation of even *your* master and mistress.

If, on the other hand, your profession of religion be not supported by consistency; if it render you proud, conceited, and consequential; if it be accompanied by an unsubdued temper, or by habits of inattention to the duties of your place; if it makes you troublesome about your religious privileges, so that in a time of emergency or sickness, you will not give up a single sermon without murmuring and sullenness, you do not glorify God, but dishonour him; you excite a prejudice against religion, rather than produce a prepossession in its favour.

Towards your fellow servants you should be meek, obliging, and generous; assuming nothing on the ground of your piety, never disgusting them by any apparent consciousness of superior sanctity, but at the same time, never scrupling to let them know and see that you fear God. Timidly to conceal your regards to the claims of religion, or vauntingly to acknowledge them, would equally excite a prejudice; but to yield to them with a firmness that ridicule and opposition cannot bend, a consistency that scrutiny cannot impeach, and a humility that the reproached conscience of those who are offended cannot misrepresent, will be sure to raise admiration, and, by the blessing of God, may produce imitation.

Are any of your fellow servants living in the neglect of religion, it is your duty, in a solemn and affectionate manner, to warn them. "I knew a religious servant," says Mr. Janeway, "that after other endeavours for the conversion of one of his fellows had proved ineffectual, spent some time at midnight to pray for him; and being very importunate, his voice was heard in the next chamber, where the object of his pious solicitude lay; who, on hearing the voice of entreaty, arose from bed to listen, and was so struck with the affectionate concern that was breathed out for him, that he was converted by the prayer."

Let me now, in conclusion, exhort you to attend to the duties which have been set before you. It may be felt as a motive to this, to consider, that though you are servants, you are not slaves, as was the case with those who are addressed by the apostles, in their inspired writings. Yes, *they* were *slaves,* and yet are they admonished to give honour and service to those who held them by a tie they could not break. You are *free,* and your labour is voluntary ; you sell it for a stipulated price, and are not degraded by your situation : nothing *can* degrade you but bad conduct. Your interest lies in the faithful discharge of your duties. This will secure to you peace and serenity of mind, the respect and attachment of your employers, the esteem of the public, the testimony of conscience, and the approbation of God. You will thus help to diffuse happiness through the families in which you reside ; for a good servant is one of the springs of domestic comfort, and daily refreshes, by its pure and pleasant stream, the members of the little community in the house; who, in return, will do what they can to promote your present comfort, and provide for your future support, when the days of sickness and the years of old age shall come upon you. And remember that God is every where, and his eye is always upon you. " He compasseth your path, and knoweth your down sitting and uprising, and there is not a word upon your tongue, but he knoweth it altogether." You may have an absent master, but you cannot have an absent God. And he cites your conscience to his side, to take a correct copy, and lodge it in your bosom, of the record of your actions, words, and feelings, which he writes down in the book of his remembrance. Time is short, life is uncertain, death is at hand, and the judgment approaching, when it will be of no consequence who was master and who was servant, but only who was holy and faithful. God is now your witness, and will be hereafter your judge. Have the promises and threatenings of the Great Master little efficacy? Are heaven, glory, and eternal happiness worth nothing? If so, what think you of condemnation, wrath, and everlasting misery? If the former signify little, do the latter signify no more? Then I must confess, I know not what further to say, for I have exhausted the differences of time, and the varieties of eternity; I have spread out the miseries which sin brings, and the pleasure which holiness produces upon earth; and have added to this the consideration of the eternal torment which iniquity draws upon itself in hell, and the everlasting felicity which religion conducts the soul to enjoy in heaven: what more *can* I add—but simply to say, choose ye, whether to you it shall be said in the last day, by the Lord Jesus Christ, "THOU WICKED AND SLOTHFUL SERVANT, DEPART ACCURSED FROM ME INTO EVERLASTING FIRE, PREPARED FOR THE DEVIL AND HIS ANGELS;" or, "WELL DONE, THOU GOOD AND FAITHFUL SERVANT, ENTER THOU INTO THE JOY OF THY LORD."

THE END.